Table of Contents

Isolated Incident
Investigating the Death of Nancy Cooper

ISBN 978-0-692-29131-3

Disclaimer: The intent of this book was to review and analyze the circumstances surrounding the death of Nancy Cooper. None of the opinions or the presentation of case information should be construed as implying anyone is guilty or innocent in the death of Nancy Cooper. The use of the word(s) "suspect" or "person of interest" does not imply someone was an official police suspect, but that the individual may have been or should have been closely reviewed regarding this case.

The conclusions drawn are not definitive, and they are based on likely outcomes rather than conclusive information. Many attempts were made to demonstrate the less than definitive nature of the information presented within this document. Wording such as, "most likely," "probably," etc. reflects the decision by the author to acknowledge deficiencies in the information around this investigation, though measures were taken to try to confirm or cross-check information.

Some of the information presented is contested by those involved. Circumstances, evidence, and investigative actions identified in this book should not be considered facts as they are based on second-hand, third-hand, or even more detached sources. Even validated sources have to be viewed skeptically, and the information presented should not be considered facts within this book. *All theories and extrapolations are the opinions of the author and should not be considered facts.*

Introduction

Contrary to most controversial murder cases, few of the facts in the murder of Nancy Cooper are in dispute. Rather, each side interpreted the facts differently. Or more precisely, they viewed them in a completely opposite manner. This case is about rush to judgment. The need for the police to assure the public everyone is safe, regardless of whether it was true or not. And with the public outraged, the police felt compelled to arrest someone quickly, and the State had to deliver a conviction.

Tragically, a young woman was murdered. She had a close-knit group of friends and family who all immediately suspected her husband, Brad Cooper, had killed her. Their suspicions were not based on facts or evidence, but based on gut feelings and a dislike for her husband. Frighteningly, the police and prosecutors applied a similar rationale. Emotion, prejudice, and gossip flowed into a courtroom and took precedence over evidence.

Brad fully cooperated with the police when Nancy was considered a missing person. Though cooperating seemed like the right thing for Brad to do, it ultimately led to his conviction. The police thought he was lying and acting strangely. Maybe only a guilty person should talk to the police, because he has nothing to lose. An innocent person has everything to lose. Unfortunately, who would not choose to help the police when his or her spouse is missing and possibly injured or worse? The very group who people should trust the most may also be who they should fear the most.

In 2006, a black, female stripper accused three white members of the Duke men's lacrosse team of rape. The accuser's statements regarding what happened were completely inconsistent. She materially changed her story several times, and many of her assertions conflicted with other statements she had made. She could not identify the perpetrators during a photo line-up, but then she later claimed her identification of the perpetrators was absolute. Two of the accused had alibis for the time of the assault. Further, a woman who accompanied the victim to the party for the Duke lacrosse players stated she was with the accuser the entire evening, and she was not aware of any sexual attack.[i]

Even though the facts of the case should have given the prosecutor plenty of reasons to question the accusations, he pursued the case aggressively. He rushed to the media. On top of his complete disregard for the facts of the case, he referenced DNA evidence that supposedly supported the rape claims, even though he knew it did not.[ii] The prosecutor conducted numerous media appearances where he helped enrage the general public by casting the Duke lacrosse players as bigoted rapists.

The case fit perfectly into several societal themes and played into many people's preconceived notions. Plus, the scene was so easy to envision. There was a group of rowdy, rich, white kids whose trust funds allowed them to attend Duke University. They were athletes who rarely attended classes and spent their time partying. One evening they paid for strippers to attend one of their drunken bashes when a few of them took things too far and raped a woman. It was so easy to see how it could have happened. However, the accusations were completely fabricated. It did not happen. In the end, the prosecutor was disbarred, but the damage was done.[iii]

In 2007, Richard Brodhead, president of Duke University stated, "The scariest thing to me is that actual human lives were at the mercy of so much instant moral certainty, before the facts had been established. If there's one lesson the world should take from the Duke lacrosse case, it's the danger of prejudgment..."[iv] Had this case gone to trial, there was little chance any of the accused would have received a fair trial. Furthermore, based on the emotions in this case, even if the facts demonstrated otherwise, the jury may have convicted. What juror wants to be considered a racist or unsympathetic to a rape victim, if they acquitted one of the lacrosse players?

Nancy's murder also fit into a conventional societal narrative, that of a weak, helpless woman murdered by a controlling husband. However, the facts did not support the narrative. The public exhibited shock and anger regarding the murder of Nancy Cooper. People wanted justice, and they wanted it quickly. *How* justice was achieved was not a primary concern. Yet, without a fair trial, we are all left just one bad circumstance away from incarceration.

Chapter 1 – Facade

July 12, 2008 (1:50 p.m.)

Operator: Cary police... how may I help you?

Caller: Hi. My name is Jessica Adam and I'm calling because a friend of mine has been missing since seven o'clock this morning and her husband and her are in the middle of a divorce... she went out for a run this morning...and no one has heard from her...

Operator: Alright and what is your friend's name?

Caller: Her, her [sic] name is Nancy Cooper...She should have been here. She was expected here no later than 9 o'clock to help me with a project and then she also had another appointment with a friend...who just called me on the other line hysterical cause she's also now having the same thought that I am about her husband, if he's done something...[v]

Jessica Adam's actions and statements set off a panic among friends, neighbors, and law enforcement even though Nancy had only been missing for less than seven hours. Tragically, Nancy Cooper was found dead two days later, her husband Brad Cooper was arrested and subsequently convicted of her murder almost three years later. Though a murder conviction usually provides finality, many questions still remained.

Nine Years Earlier

In a happier time, Brad Cooper and Nancy Rentz met while working at the technology company TransCanada Pipelines in Calgary, Canada in the 1990's. Brad was quiet and soft-spoken, a classic introvert. He was tall and lean, but muscular. Nancy was beautiful with an athletic build. However, it was Nancy's personality that drew the most attention. Nancy was the life of the party, but she was also a great listener. She made friends easily. Everyone wanted to be around her. Nancy was fun and perky, constantly engaging people. She was the opposite of Brad, but somehow they worked. Brad proposed in late 1999 and upon Nancy's acceptance, a wedding was planned for 2001. In the interim, Brad received a job offer from Cisco Systems in North Carolina. In order for Nancy to be able to move with him, they had to be married. As a result, Brad and Nancy exchanged vows in a small, quickly-arranged wedding in October of 2000, which facilitated their joint move to the United States.[vi]

Brad and Nancy Cooper moved from Canada to a suburb of Raleigh, North Carolina. Raleigh is the state capital with a metropolitan area of over one million people. It is a diverse mix of people born and raised in the South and transplants from all over the world, though most seem to have migrated from larger, northeastern cities. Raleigh sits adjacent to Durham and in between them is the heavily bio-technology region called Research Triangle Park or RTP. RTP is home to numerous research organizations, pharmaceutical companies, and technology companies of all sizes. Cisco's main campus for the Raleigh region is located in RTP.

Not far from RTP is the town of Cary, which was where Brad and Nancy called home. Cary is a suburb of Raleigh, but in a way, it is self-contained. It has a population of over 100,000 people, composed mostly of new arrivals to the Raleigh-Durham area. Cary is more pretentious than the surrounding areas, but its ostentatious reputation is more a source of pride than an insult. As of 2011, Cary had a median household income of $82,509 while the surrounding area hovered closer to $50,000.[vii] Along with greater income and wealth, Cary resembles the Northeast more than the South. Many of its residents are from the Northeast and bring with them their views on the importance of maintaining outward appearances and outdoing your neighbors.

The Coopers' purchased a home in the Lochmere area of Cary. For those who love the pretentious nature of Cary, Lochmere serves as an advanced version with its large homes and beautiful lakes. Cary is a beautiful small city where children can play and adults can enjoy life without the crime associated with a larger city. Cary regularly ranked as one of the safest communities in the country. As a result, Cary real estate garners a premium and is highly sought out by new-comers to the area.

From all outward appearances, the Coopers had a normal and healthy relationship when they arrived in North Carolina, and for many years this was seemingly the case. After several unfortunate miscarriages, the Coopers had two girls: Isabella, referred to as Bella, born in 2004, and Gabriella, referred to as Katie, born in 2006. Right around the time Katie was born Brad and Nancy's relationship hit the rocks. Their problems were openly acknowledged by both. Whether the initial tension was a result of money, children, or differences, the couple's dynamic changed for the worse. Nancy stopped having sex with Brad.[viii] Brad was focused on his career and training for triathlons while Nancy was left to take care of the house and children.

Nancy continued to make friends while Brad traveled and advanced his career. Their interests moved in different directions. They were no longer planning activities together. Brad would use his free time to work out while Nancy expanded her social network and found ways to have fun while also caring for the girls.

Though unknown to Brad at the time, Nancy had at least two affairs during their marriage. During the summer of 2001, Nancy confessed to a friend that she had an affair while she was in Florida on vacation with her sister Jill. Nancy claimed to be in love with this man and continued the relationship for some time.[ix] In 2005, while Brad was out of town for business, a neighbor by the name of John Pearson walked Nancy home from a Halloween party. They were accompanied by the Cooper's neighbors, Craig and Diana Duncan. After the Duncans entered their house across the street, John and Nancy went inside her house. They proceeded to have sex, though John was unable to remember many details as a result of his high level of intoxication.[x] Nancy has allegedly had other affairs, but they are unsubstantiated.

In late 2004, Brad also engaged in infidelity. He had an affair with Heather Metour, one of Nancy's closest friends. Nancy suspected Brad of having other affairs, but Heather was the only one Brad admitted to her. Both spouses were seeking outside relationships as a means of coping with their marital problems.

Years later, Heather felt compelled to tell Nancy about the affair as an attempt to ease her guilt or possibly punish Brad and/or Nancy. Maybe it was a sort of societal karma, but Heather was later sued for alienation of affection for having an affair with another married man who happened to be the same John Pearson with whom Nancy had an affair. Nancy confronted Brad about the affair, and as usually happens when there are affairs, he lied. Brad acted shocked and dismayed at the accusation. Brad denied the affair for almost a year.[xi] Nancy believed the affair was true and treated Brad accordingly. In early 2008, Brad came forward and acknowledged the affair to Nancy. Initially, he denied the affair with the hope of saving the marriage, but ultimately decided they had to face it.

In February of 2008, they entered couples' therapy, but Nancy quickly withdrew from the sessions. She was not able to move past the affair.[xii] Though Nancy had also been unfaithful, she could not accept Brad's indiscretion. Maybe she saw it as a betrayal she could not forgive, or it was the excuse she had been looking for to end the marriage. Either way, Brad's affair set the wheels in motion toward separation and most likely divorce.

Though the affairs were secret throughout most of the marriage, the family spending was out in the open. The couples' chronic spending, led primarily by Nancy, drove the family deep into debt. Whether Nancy needed to *keep up with the Joneses* or the spending was a means for her to cope with underlying issues, she spent well beyond the family's resources.

In 2007, Nancy spent over $27,000 on her American Express credit card alone.[xiii] At the time, Brad was making around $100,000 - $120,000/year, while Nancy was unable to work due to her immigration status. Nancy purchased a painting of a bear for more than $8,000. In October of 2007, Nancy had Brad purchase her a $3,000 diamond pendant necklace though she really wanted a $7,000 necklace.[xiv] *This necklace later became a factor in Brad's murder trial as many of Nancy's friends claimed she never took it off.* For Christmas, Nancy bought Brad a $12,000 Louis Vuitton laptop case, which he later returned. Nancy drove a fully-loaded 2004 BMW X5 sport utility vehicle, and Brad drove a 2001 BMW 325i. The Coopers belonged to a fitness club (Lifetime Fitness) and a local swimming pool. The girls attended a private pre-school. Though some of the spending was reasonable for their level of income, most greatly exceeded their means. Regardless, appearances were maintained.

According to Brad, the Coopers' credit card debt reached $45,000. He attributed most of the debt to Nancy's spending. Nancy's parents claimed Brad lied about how much Nancy spent.[xv] Nancy's mother Donna claimed Nancy primarily spent money on food. She was forced to use credit cards for all spending because she had no access to the family money. Nevertheless, as if to refute her own statements, Donna stated that they (Nancy's parents) had given Nancy and Brad $25,000 to help with credit card debt.[xvi] If Nancy was spending within the means of the family, why did Nancy's parents have to give them tens of thousands of dollars? Nancy's father, Garry, knew of an $80,000 home equity line his daughter and Brad took out in order to pay off credit card debt as well. The Cooper's financial distress was not a secret within the family.

To counter the excessive spending, they also borrowed against Brad's 401(K) to cover monthly expenditures. Clearly, the family had a spending problem. The massive accumulated debt was not because Nancy could not get access to money; it was because there was no money. It had all been spent. Nancy and Brad had spent beyond their means and beyond their savings. The only option was to go deeper in debt.

Brad initially tried talking to Nancy about her spending. He emphasized the need to spend within their means. This approached failed dismally. Nancy kept her spending in check, until she felt like spending, which was often. Next, Brad provided Nancy with a separate checking account. He deposited money into the account and Nancy could withdraw money through her debit card. This arrangement provided Nancy with an alternative money source. It was designed to stop Nancy from using credit cards and to limit her spending. Unfortunately, Nancy could not limit her spending. She overdrew the account several times.[xvii] The spending control measure did not have its desired effect. It merely caused an additional problem as they had to contend with an overdrawn bank account. The financial constraints did not successfully control Nancy's activities as she spent like a woman with a trust fund.

Finally, in the early part of 2008, Brad placed Nancy on a specific budget. Prior to this budget, Nancy did pretty much whatever she wanted. She went out with friends to dinners and parties. She shopped; she spent. She took numerous vacations each year. Nancy's spending drove the family toward financial ruin, but it did not slow her down. Picking up the tab for others at dinner was a way for Nancy to show how much money they had. Even though they were deeply in debt, Nancy still tried to convey the image of wealth.

For Nancy, everything in her life was manageable until Brad clamped down on her finances. Maybe Brad put Nancy on a budget as retribution for her seeking a divorce, or it may have been out of pure necessity. Regardless, the timing of the change was suspect, given the close proximity to Nancy's decision to separate; however, the budget constraints were long overdue. Though Brad may have been a spender too, Nancy seemed to thrive on it. Spending was a distraction from whatever Nancy chose to bury emotionally. Further, she loved status. Nancy wanted people to think she had money. It was important to her.

Under the new budget, Nancy would no longer have access to the bank accounts or credit cards, as her spending had materially impacted the financial health of the family. Nancy could not be trusted with money. According to Brad's deposition, each month after all the bills were paid there was approximately $1,300 left from his pay checks. He gave Nancy $300/week or $1,200/month to cover groceries, gas, going out, and other miscellaneous items. This left Brad with only $100/month or $25/week. If the girls or Nancy needed something additional, she would discuss it with Brad. He would provide her with additional money if he thought the purchase was necessary.[xviii]

Though the budgeted amount for Nancy of $300/week seemed more than reasonable given the circumstances, it infuriated Nancy. It could have been $1,000/week; it still would have gotten the same reaction from Nancy. Brad constrained Nancy, and she did not like it. Though little was heard of Nancy's complaints prior to early 2008, once the "Budget Nazi," Nancy's nickname for Brad, put his foot down, she screamed from the roof-tops. Anyone and everyone who would listen to Nancy heard about the financial controls her husband had placed on her.

Nancy never mentioned the financial peril she had driven the family toward. She never mentioned money prior to the budget unless it was in reference to something she bought or contemplated buying. Now, everything had changed. Most likely, Nancy was trying to pressure Brad into eliminating the budget by getting friends aligned against him. Though Nancy always had a reputation for embellishing stories, once she felt wronged, all bets were off. No longer could her statements be viewed as mere exaggerations. She misled people in order to garner sympathy and support. Nancy despised Brad for curtailing her lifestyle. By setting limits on her spending, Nancy could not do what she wanted. She had to be financially accountable, and she wanted no part of it.

The imposed budget marked a significant negative turning point in the relationship of Brad and Nancy Cooper. The period lasted until her death. Brad had essentially forced Nancy to go cold turkey regarding her addiction to spending and shopping. She had no outlet for her shopping vice. It was as if someone threw an alcoholic into a room and prevented her from having even a single drink. And the room had a window to the person's friends in order for her to vent her frustrations and receive sympathy for the pains she was enduring. Unlike alcoholism, a person addicted to shopping/spending does not have the same level of acceptance and understanding, though the consequences and impact are very similar.

With Nancy's spending significantly curtailed, she turned her attention toward separating from Brad. Brad still loved Nancy and wanted to work things out. However, Brad appeared to accept that the marriage was coming to an end. Much like many aspects of Nancy and Brad's relationship, the plan for separation and divorce was strained, but progressing. Initially, everyone planned to move back to Canada. The girls would live with Nancy while Brad worked and lived nearby. It seemed like a reasonable plan whereby Nancy could be closer to her family and Brad would still be able to spend time with the girls. This was the plan until Nancy's attorney, Alice Stubbs, drafted a separation agreement in preparation for the upcoming divorce.

A separation agreement is a contract between husband and wife, which outlines the conditions (alimony, child support, mortgage payments, asset division, and other obligations) surrounding separation prior to divorce. Though a separation agreement is not the divorce agreement, many times it is incorporated into the divorce agreement. Getting both parties to sign a separation agreement usually enables the divorce process to go more smoothly, as major decisions are made well before the actual divorce takes place. It is also where a lot of problems can percolate, since some people chose to either ask for too much or let their emotions bleed into the agreement. This is where a good divorce attorney can mitigate a lot of the conflict and stress of divorce. Most seasoned divorce attorneys understand that ending up in court during a divorce is rarely in their client's best interest. It is emotionally and financially devastating. Only the attorneys benefit from a courtroom battle, as a result of the substantial fees collected. In the end, one has to defer the critical decisions to a judge who will likely distribute the assets equitably. Therefore, a separation agreement should be reasonable to the other side, even if the other side does not completely agree with what is being requested.

Nancy's attorney, Alice Stubbs, drafted a one-sided separation agreement where it appeared the intent was to incite Brad, not foster an atmosphere of negotiation. When one is faced with losing everything, he has no choice but to fight. Nancy's attorney created an environment where Brad had nothing to lose by pushing back. At the time, the spouses were working things out. They had a plan; however, Nancy's attorney made a significant strategic error, which ended the amicable discussions regarding the separation. Not only did Nancy not get what she wanted in the agreement, Ms. Stubbs destroyed the plans Nancy already had. The demands in the agreement were so egregious to Brad that he called off the move to Canada and told Nancy he now needed to speak to an attorney.

The separation agreement provided for Nancy to have physical custody of both Bella and Katie in Canada. Brad had been unable to find a job in Canada as of the time of the agreement, which meant the terms of the agreement removed the girls from his daily life. Per the agreement, Brad could see the girls every other weekend, but he was required to pay for all travel, whether it was for him to travel to Canada or for Nancy and the girls to come to North Carolina. Brad could also see the girls for two non-consecutive weeks in the summer.[xix] If Nancy moved to Canada without Brad, he would essentially be unable to see his daughters on any consistent basis. It would have been very costly and time prohibitive for him to spend time with Bella and Katie. Though moving to Canada may have been easier on Nancy, it would have deprived the girls of their father.

From an emotional stand-point, the separation from his daughters would have created a tremendous amount of stress on Brad, even though he spent much of his time at work. The separation arrangement also placed a significant financial strain on him, as it required an extensive outflow of money if he wanted to spend time with his daughters. The drafted agreement also addressed the financial distribution of the income and assets, which did little to alleviate Brad's concerns about the future.

Per the agreement, the Cooper house was to be sold. The proceeds from the sale were to be utilized to pay off the mortgage(s), and any remaining funds would be used to pay off Nancy's car loan. Further, any remaining monies from the sale of the house would go toward the 401(K) loan and then credit card debts. If any money remained, all of it would go to Nancy. Nancy would have also received all of the funds from Brad's 401(K). Along with Nancy receiving all of the assets, the separation agreement provided for Brad to assume all of the debts.[xx]

At the time of the Coopers' separation, Brad's income was approximately $105,000.[xxi] After state and federal income taxes, social security, Medicare, 401(K) contributions, and the employee portion of any benefits, Brad's take-home pay was approximately $5,000 - $6,000/month. Brad also received bonuses, but unlike salary, the bonuses were discretionary and fluctuated based on company and individual performance.

The separation agreement provided for $2,100 a month in child support, which was likely tied to a set formula. On top of the child support, the agreement required Brad to pay for several other items on behalf of the girls. He was required to pay for private schools for the girls until the end of high school, which amounted to over $2,000/month.[xxii] It further provided that Brad pay for all extra-curricular activities and clothes for his girls, adding at least another several hundred dollars a month, to the required expenditures. Brad was also to pay for all health and dental insurance premiums for his girls and Nancy, as well as cover any expenses not covered by insurance. Depending on the circumstances, expenses not covered by insurance could have been anywhere from minimal to catastrophic in any given month. Since they would be divorced it was very unlikely Brad's work insurance policy would have covered Nancy. As a result, Brad would have had to purchase additional dental and medical insurance policies for Nancy, on top of adding the girls to his individual policies. Brad was further required to pay all of his own life insurance policies and have Nancy as his sole beneficiary.

Without accounting for Brad's taking even one trip to visit his daughters or alimony, the separation agreement Ms.

Stubbs drafted likely allotted more money to Nancy than Brad brought home in a given month. The agreement also called for alimony for eight years, but left the dollar amount blank. It was not clear where Ms. Stubbs was going to find the funds to support her next request for additional monies from Brad.

Determination of alimony in the state of North Carolina takes many factors into consideration, such as economic/career sacrifices by a dependent spouse, standard of living, and infidelity of one or both parties, to name a few. Nancy had informed Ms. Stubbs of Brad's affair with Heather Metour and alluded to others. However, she neglected to inform Ms. Stubbs of her own indiscretions, which Brad may have been unaware of at the time. Though Brad's affair could have cost him dearly, if Nancy had also engaged in infidelity, the court may have significantly reduced or eliminated her alimony award. Regardless of the direction the divorce may have taken, Ms. Stubbs took a relatively amicable separation and turned it into a contentious situation, where at the very least it kept her client from returning home to Canada.

Nancy's last email to Alice Stubbs was on April 29, 2008. There were no emails between the two of them in May, June, or July of 2008.[xxiii] Communication had almost ceased. There were two phone calls between Nancy and Alice during those few months, but each lasted only a couple of minutes.[xxiv] It was not clear why Nancy stopped contacting her attorney. She continued to tell her friends and family that the marriage was over. She and Brad continued to argue. Nevertheless, Brad's opinion on the state of the marriage differed significantly from Nancy's friends and family. He thought things had gotten better and maybe there was a chance at reconciliation.[xxv]

After Brad admitted to the affair, he knew that keeping the marriage together was an uphill battle. He made changes in an attempt to improve their relationship. He worked fewer hours. He started getting more involved in the girls' lives, and he began helping around the house.[xxvi] It may have been too little, too late, but it was his attempt at making things better. After years of wanting Brad around more, Nancy did not react favorably to Brad's new focus on the family. She felt he hovered. He felt he was being a good father and husband.

Though Nancy provided no clue to her friends or family of a change in her decision regarding divorce, Brad's opinion and her lack of correspondence with her attorney indicated otherwise. Nancy may have been trying to manipulate Brad into thinking reconciliation was possible so that she could get what she wanted: divorced, but with sufficient money to sustain her lifestyle. Nancy was playing one side, and it was most likely Brad.

Nancy wrote an email to her father titled, "I need help." In the email she stated, "Brad is going a little crazy. He had my water cut off."[xxvii] Even though Nancy was in her mid-30s, she looked to her father for help. Nonetheless, this would upset and alarm almost any father regardless of the circumstances. Was his son-in-law going crazy? Why did he cut off his own wife's water? The message was clear: Brad was losing it and Nancy was scared.

Yet, the facts did not support this conclusion. When her friends asked, Nancy specifically stated that she was not afraid of Brad. There was another problem with the content of her email. Though it was literally close to the truth, it was deceptive in nature. Brad did not have the water cut off. He failed to pay the water bill.

During 2007, there were several occasions where the water bill was either paid late or disconnected.[xxviii] Brad was responsible for paying the bills, and clearly his track record was dismal. He appeared disorganized and forgetful. In early 2008, Brad had forgotten to pay the water bill again, and he apparently missed the subsequent notification in the mail. Since Nancy was taken off of the checking account and she had no credit cards, when she discovered the water had been shut off, she was unable to turn it back on. This infuriated her and resulted in the above mentioned email to her father. She also called Brad at work, at which time he had the water turned back on. Did Brad do this on purpose? If so, what was the point? He still lived at the house. He turned the water back on as soon as he became aware of the situation. As with the previous times, he likely just forgot.

Nancy knew Brad was bad at paying bills on time. However, she was very upset by the fact that she could not fix the problem because Brad had taken away her financial independence. This was likely what spurred her anger. However, why did she email her dad as if to indicate she was in a dire situation? What was her goal? She could have just been very emotional and needed to vent, though Nancy had to know what affect her email would have on her father.

In some states, protective/restraining orders specifically identify shutting off utilities as a violation of the order. Was Nancy setting the stage for trying to seek a protective order, maybe as a way to evict Brad from the house or gain an advantage in the divorce? Nancy indirectly conveyed a fear of Brad, yet when asked, she always said she was not afraid of him. Was Nancy playing both sides? The discrepancies in Nancy's statements and actions toward Brad, compared to what she conveyed to her friends and family, would soon have a very detrimental effect on Brad's believability in the eyes of law enforcement.

Chapter 2 - The Week Prior

In late June of 2008, Nancy and the girls went on vacation with Nancy's parents, sister, and brother-in-law. They first went to a lake near Charlotte, North Carolina and then headed to Hilton Head, South Carolina. During the trip, Nancy made it clear to her family that her relationship with Brad was over. Brad did not join the family on vacation. Brad stayed home and worked; however, he and Nancy spoke 20 times during that week.[xxix] Though Nancy told her family that divorce was inevitable, it was not as clear what she said to Brad during their numerous phone calls. Brad and Nancy continued to have some form of a relationship.

Near the end of the vacation, Brad called Nancy to brag about cleaning the house.[xxx] While the family vacationed, Brad spent most of his time working. Yet, he did manage to clean a little and wanted Nancy to know what he had done.

When they returned home from the vacation the week before Nancy's death, she was terribly upset with the condition of the house. So much so, that she complained to friends about the condition of the house. It was a mess, there was no food for the girls to eat, and the kitchen was covered with bugs. Nancy left her father a voicemail complaining about the condition of the house, though it was not clear what her objective was in making the call.

Brad apparently cleaned some of the house while the family was on vacation, but either his efforts fell far short of Nancy's expectations or the areas he cleaned were out-weighed by the areas he neglected. Based on Nancy's rants,

Brad's cleaning was highly ineffective. Brad vacuumed the house, dusted, and cleaned the kitchen, but he apparently chose not to clean the dishes in the sink.[xxxi] Nancy was known to exaggerate, but most likely Brad was terrible at cleaning. *During the trial, the prosecution presented information indicating Brad was so good at cleaning that the best forensics in the world could not find even a trace of his having killed Nancy.* What Brad thought was clean Nancy considered an utter disaster area. Nancy's return from vacation was not the rekindling of their relationship Brad had hoped. He was even more in the doghouse now.

Nancy's numerous comments to friends regarding the condition of the home were likely generally accurate, but provided without context. Failure to provide context seemed to be a trademark of Nancy. For example, the Coopers had been dealing with an ongoing infestation issue for years, and most bugs and insects are much more prevalent in the summer months. Therefore, the fact there were bugs in the kitchen when she returned from vacation was far less dramatic than what it would imply without understanding the baseline.

Brad also did not go to the grocery store the previous week. As a result, Nancy had to shop for food after returning from her vacation. Not the most desirable task, but most people have to grocery shop after they return from vacation. It would have been nice if Brad had picked up groceries for the family prior to their arrival, but he either did not have the time or it did not occur to him. Regardless, Nancy complained. Brad, who worked all week, did not run errands for her while she had been on vacation. It is hard to imagine many people garnering sympathy for Brad, if the roles were reversed and he went on vacation while Nancy stayed home to work. Regardless, Nancy's complaints about Brad garnered her tremendous sympathy within her network of friends.

The week leading up to Nancy's death deviated little from a relatively normal week for the Coopers. Brad worked and Nancy stayed at home with the girls. On Monday, July 7, 2008, Nancy contacted the exterminator, Gary Beard, to address the bug situation. Mr. Beard visited the Cooper residence the following day. He sprayed the house, but only found ants in the kitchen. As would become more critical during the trial phase, Mr. Beard checked the rest of the house and observed the garage was just as cluttered as it was during other visits to the Cooper's residence.[xxxii]

To earn extra money and help her friend, Nancy had agreed to paint a room in Jessica Adam's house. On Tuesday morning after dropping the girls off at pre-school, Nancy headed to Jessica's house to paint. During the evening, Nancy went to Jennifer Fetterolf's house, while Brad watched the girls.[xxxiii]

Nancy also painted at Jessica's on Wednesday until around 1:30 p.m., when she picked the girls up from pre-school.[xxxiv] On Wednesday evening, Nancy, Brad, and the girls went to Mike and Clea Morwick's house. While at the Morwick's, Nancy claimed she was not feeling well. She left Brad to watch the girls and instead of going home, Nancy returned to Jessica's house.[xxxv]

On Thursday, Nancy went for a long run. During the day, Nancy spoke to her neighbor Diana Duncan outside her house. She also talked to Jennifer Fetterolf on the phone. During the conversation, Nancy mentioned a cookout at the Duncan residence the following evening, but she did not mention any other weekend plans.[xxxvi]

On Friday, July 11, at 5:20 a.m., Nancy called her friend, Carey Clark, to cancel their scheduled run that morning. They were supposed to run eight miles at a local state park, William B. Umstead Park. Nancy told Carey her legs were tired from running the day prior, and she planned to do a weight routine at the gym later in the morning.[xxxvii] Nancy also called Jessica Adam sometime in the morning, and they *supposedly* discussed plans to meet at Nancy's house later in the day.[xxxviii]

Nancy called Brad several times during the afternoon, but she was unable to reach him. Brad had not provided Nancy with her weekly allowance of $300, which she usually received on Fridays. There was some debate regarding the allowance as to whether Brad forgot, or he chose not to give her an allowance because of the money she received from her parents during vacation and the money she received from painting. Once they finally spoke, Brad offered to leave work and bring her the money, but Nancy declined.[xxxix]

During the afternoon while Brad worked, Nancy took Bella and Katie to the local pool. On the way home from the pool, they stopped at the grocery store, Harris Teeter, to pick up food items for the Duncan's cookout later in the evening. From the grocery store, Nancy and the girls went home. Nancy had to prepare for the party. She was cooking ribs and pulling various food dishes together in order to take them to the Duncan's house across the street. At around 5:00

p.m., Nancy spoke to Jessica Adam on the phone, though later Jessica stated that she went over to the Cooper house instead of talking on the phone. Other than Jessica's statements, there was no corroborating information indicating Jessica was in the Cooper residence on July 11. Nonetheless, Jessica provided the police with extensive information regarding what she saw in the Cooper house on the evening before Nancy's disappearance.

Nancy and the girls arrived at the Duncan residence around 6:00 p.m. After leaving work around the same time, Brad stopped by Lowe's Food on his way to the party to purchase beer. He arrived at the Duncan's house around 7:00 p.m. The Duncan's backyard and house were filled with neighbors and friends who were eating, drinking, and talking while the kids played. When Brad arrived Nancy conveyed her displeasure with his failure to give her the weekly allowance. Several attendees at the party described this discussion as an argument, though most saw it as one-sided with Nancy much more upset than Brad.[xl] Nancy ended her diatribe by placing Brad in charge of the girls while she socialized. Brad ate a little food and pushed the girls on the swings. He took the girls home around 8:00 p.m. Brad read to the girls and got them ready for bed around 9:00 p.m. The girls slept in the guest room with him, as he and Nancy had been sleeping in separate rooms for months.[xli]

After Brad left the party, Nancy began to relax. Nancy had been drinking throughout the evening, which also likely contributed to her calming. Several attendees described Nancy as buzzed, but not drunk. According to Diana Duncan, who hosted the party, Nancy consumed four glasses of wine and then switched to beer during the evening.[xlii] Being a relatively thin woman, if she consumed five or more alcoholic beverages, Nancy likely exceeded most definitions of intoxication.

Nancy spoke to several people throughout the evening. Her primary topic was the couple's relationship and the financial unfairness of her situation. Upon meeting a party attendee, Donna Lopez, for the first time, Nancy told her about Brad's affair and other personal details about her marital relationship. Nancy explained to Donna that she had to sometimes walk many places with a backpack because she did not have a car.[xliii] Donna took this statement to mean Nancy currently did not have a car and was forced to walk around Cary with two small girls in order to buy groceries and make doctor's appointments. Though this was likely the message Nancy tried to convey, it was a stretch on reality. Nancy had a car, but at one point in the past she did not have a car because she wanted to wait for a specially-ordered, fully-loaded car. The Coopers only had one car for a short period of time because of Nancy's decision. Nancy twisted the facts in a manner to garner additional sympathy from unsuspecting new-comers to her circle.

Later in the evening, Mike Hiller, a family friend, approached Nancy and asked her when he would be able to play tennis with Brad. Understanding the dynamic between Brad and Nancy, Mike knew to approach Nancy to get approval for Brad to play tennis. Nancy took out her cell phone and dialed Brad. She told Mike to ask Brad himself. In Nancy's presence, Mike and Brad agreed to play tennis the following morning at 9:30 a.m. while Nancy agreed to watch the girls.[xliv]

Around 10:50 p.m., Jessica Adam called Nancy from her husband's cell phone. This was the last call received on Nancy's cell phone prior to her disappearance.[xlv] Jessica asked Nancy to come over. Nancy declined, indicating she had too much to drink for her to be driving. A couple of hours later, around 12:30 a.m. Nancy went home. She looked in on her girls, and then crashed onto her bed, exhausted from the day.

Chapter 3 – Tragedy Strikes

On the morning of July 12, 2008, the Cooper's youngest daughter Katie woke up around 4:00 a.m. Brad took Katie downstairs to avoid waking Bella. Nancy came downstairs wearing only a white t-shirt around 4:30 a.m. It was one of Brad's t-shirts.[xlvi] Women usually wear the clothes of a boyfriend or husband not just because they liked the clothing item or found it comfortable, but because it demonstrated that she cared. She wanted to be close to him. Nevertheless, Brad and Nancy were in the middle of a somewhat heated and contested situation. Nancy told friends how much she hated Brad. If so, why was she wearing his t-shirt?

Nancy may have found Brad's shirt comfortable and convenient, but if Nancy wanted to show Brad how much she hated him she would not have worn his shirt. Most likely, Nancy wore his shirt as an indicator to Brad that she still cared about him on some level. She likely wanted to divorce Brad. She may have even hated him at times, but Nancy actively managed people's perceptions to her advantage. Nancy may have yelled at Brad and refused to sleep with him, but she also countered those actions with enough niceties for him to think there may still have been a chance they might get back together. If for any other reason, keeping Brad smitten helped maintain civility in the relationship. In addition, she wanted out; however, she wanted money too.

Throughout the relationship, Nancy was able to get Brad to do just about whatever she wanted. If she was out with friends and had too much to drink, she would call Brad to come get them. She knew he would do it. If she wanted to buy something expensive, she would convince Brad the purchase was necessary. And she was successful many times, as was demonstrated by the family's considerable debts and large quantity of possessions. This was the dynamic of their relationship until Brad imposed "the budget." Nancy was absolutely livid with Brad for reigning in her spending and in essence, cutting off her freedom. Nancy's anger toward Brad became obvious to everyone, probably even Brad. Yet, in private, Nancy most likely still provided Brad with hints and suggestions that they had a chance as a couple. Nancy knew how to keep Brad interested and the white t-shirt was just another example.

As Nancy made her way downstairs, she and Brad tried to soothe Katie while straightening up the house. A little before 6:00 a.m. Nancy asked Brad to go to the grocery store to get milk, as there was none in the house. Nancy held Brad responsible for the lack of milk in the house, since he did not grocery shop while she and the girls were on vacation the week prior. Thus, Brad drove to Harris Teeter to buy the milk. Brad had barely taken off his shoes upon returning home from the grocery store, and Nancy sent him back to the store to buy laundry detergent.[xlvii] While on the drive, Nancy called Brad to ask him to also purchase green juice for the girls. After Brad returned home from the grocery store a second time, he went upstairs to work on the computer. He reviewed emails while holding Katie on his lap. Around 7:00 a.m. Nancy yelled to Brad from the first floor asking for a specific running top. Before Brad got up to help her find the clothing item, he heard the front door shut, indicating she had left for her run.[xlviii]

Shortly after Nancy left, Brad put Katie back to bed. He returned to surfing the Internet and reviewing emails until about 8:30 a.m. when Bella awoke. Brad took Bella downstairs and fed her breakfast. After breakfast, Brad and Bella watched television, until Katie awoke around 9:00 a.m. Brad fed Katie and then played some games with her. Around this time, Brad left a voicemail for Mike Hiller informing him Nancy had yet to return from her run; therefore, their tennis match may be delayed. Mike called Brad back letting him know he would have to cancel their tennis match because he had another match scheduled at 11:00 a.m. At this point, Brad felt Nancy was punishing him by not returning from her run in time for him to play tennis. Since Nancy was already upset with him because of the condition of the house upon her return from vacation, Brad decided to clean.[xlix] Though Brad had also cleaned and done laundry while the family was on vacation, it was nonetheless a rare occurrence.

Around 9:30 a.m., Jessica Adam called the Cooper's home phone asking for Nancy. Brad informed Jessica that Nancy had gone running with Carey Clark.[l] It was not clear why Brad thought she was running with Carey, as Nancy had not told him she was running with Carey or anyone else for that matter. Nancy left the house around two and half hours prior, and he may have made the conclusion about running with Carey merely based on the length of time Nancy had been gone. Plus, Nancy had cancelled her run with Carey the day prior, and they could have rescheduled the run for today.

Once Brad missed his tennis match, he decided to clean the floors in an attempt to make Nancy happy. He spent the remainder of the morning cleaning, doing laundry, and taking care of the girls, which were all activities new to Brad since he recently started making an effort to help out more around the house.[li]

Though she expressed no concern to Brad during the earlier call, around noon Jessica began calling Nancy's friends and neighbors. Jessica conveyed a message of, "Nancy seems to be missing." It was as if she was getting the word out of Nancy's disappearance rather than simply looking for Nancy. She did not try to directly call Nancy on her cell phone, but she let others know she was worried.

By late morning, Brad was concerned. Brad's annoyance with Nancy's long absence turned into worry. Maybe Nancy had gone to lunch with a friend, but she did not have her cell phone or wallet. Brad called Jessica Adam in order to locate Carey Clark's phone number. He still believed she may have gone running with her. Another friend of Nancy's, Hannah Prichard, called looking for Nancy. Brad also asked Hannah if she had Carey's phone number, but neither of them knew Carey's number. Shortly after 1:00 p.m. Brad told Jessica he was going to put the girls in the car and look for Nancy. Jessica offered to watch the girls, but Brad declined. Brad and the girls circled the neighborhood; drove past where Carey lived; and even stopped at Nancy's gym, Lifetime Fitness.[lii] No one had seen Nancy.

With Nancy gone for less than seven hours, Jessica Adam frantically called the Cary Police Department to report her friend missing. Jessica claimed Nancy was supposed to be at her house at 8:00 a.m. in the morning to paint. Jessica was breathless and panicked as she spoke to the police. Though she did eventually convey the fact that Nancy was missing, Jessica spent most of the conversation alluding to the idea Brad had hurt Nancy in some capacity. Jessica did not provide the police with Nancy's phone number or complete physical description, but she did mention divorce three times. After the call to law enforcement, Jessica raced over to the Cooper residence with another friend, Mary Anderson. She arrived before the police.

Jessica waited for police to arrive, followed by Brad and his girls. As the neighbors began to gather in front of the Cooper house, Jessica began, not so discreetly, conveying her theory regarding Nancy's mysterious disappearance. *She was badly hurt or dead, and Brad was responsible.* Her comments were loud enough for Brad to hear, as well as most of the other people who gathered. Jessica pushed hard to get friends to go along with her theory of Brad's involvement in Nancy's disappearance.[liii] If someone did not agree with her opinions, she did not want to speak to them. When Mike Hiller (who Brad was supposed to play tennis with earlier) arrived, he immediately questioned Jessica's story regarding Nancy's plans to paint at her house earlier in the morning. He spoke to Nancy the night prior, and he knew Nancy had agreed to stay home with the girls while he and Brad played tennis at 9:30 a.m. In response, Jessica informed Mike he was not to speak to the police unless it was through her.[liv]

During the afternoon, Jessica was hysterical. Brad's neighbor, Craig Duncan, described her as being in a "frightful panic."[lv] Jessica's emotions, coupled with her statements about what likely happened to Nancy, received considerable notice from those gathered. Many of the gathered friends and neighbors began to suspect Brad of wrong-doing. It was only hours after Nancy's disappearance, but the story's arc had already been created. Suddenly, all of Brad's actions or inactions were indicators of guilt. Everything he did implicated him further.

Clea Morwick, a friend of Nancy's, called Nancy's twin sister Krista Lister in Canada to tell her Nancy was missing. Similar to those gathered outside the Cooper house, Krista immediately suspected Brad had done something to Nancy. She hung up with Clea and called Brad. Krista asked Brad where Nancy was. Brad stated he did not know. After a couple rounds of questions and answers, Krista cut to the chase and demanded to know what he had done to her! Brad hung up on her. Though Krista later described his demeanor as sad on the call, she still suspected he had done something to her sister.[lvi]

Though Brad's naturally quiet and peculiar personality may have been a hindrance to him much of his life, on this day it became detrimental. Society rewards extroverts and out-going personalities. There are few accolades associated with being introspective; and unfortunately, Brad is quite the introvert. And the very attributes people used to describe Brad in general, now became signs of guilt with Nancy missing. Diana Duncan thought it was strange that Brad would not look up, though Brad commonly avoided eye contact.[lvii] Craig Duncan observed Brad as emotionless, though Brad rarely exhibited emotion.[lviii]

Brad being Brad was now problematic. Add to this, many friends and neighbors were openly expressing opinions that Brad may have done something to Nancy. As a result of Brad hearing these allegations, he further distanced himself from the group. Additionally, Brad was juggling questions from the police, dealing with the care of two young girls and trying to find his missing wife. What his behavior *should have been* is somewhat subjective and different for everyone. Each person responds differently to stress. Some people cry. Some people get angry. And some people hold it in. None of these reactions should have caused alarm.

If Brad acted like Nancy was already dead, it would have been concerning. However, Brad's actions and statements demonstrated that he was actively looking for Nancy and assisting with trying to find her. Yet, Jessica Adam found Brad's actions strange. He wore a baseball cap and he did not approach her, even though she repeatedly stated that she thought he had done something to Nancy.[lix] Nancy was the darling of the neighborhood and Brad was the mean husband; therefore, it did not take much for most people to turn on Brad. He realized quickly that he had few friends whom he could trust. Because of Krista's call, Brad also knew Nancy's family thought he had done something to her as well. Brad and his limited social skills were all he had to counter the gathering mob.

Nancy had been actively battling Brad's affair and budget restrictions in the court of public opinion for months while Brad sat quietly. Though Nancy's goals were most likely to get Brad to relent on her budget and to garner sympathy from those around her, she turned Brad into a villain and herself into a victim. With Nancy missing, she truly was a victim, and with Brad remaining suspiciously quiet, he validated his role as villain.

On the evening of July 14, Brad made a public statement for the first and only time. Brad stepped before the media wearing a long-sleeve, white button shirt and a Cisco baseball cap. Brad asked anyone who had information on Nancy's disappearance to come forward. He also thanked the many volunteers who had helped look for Nancy. He did not answer any questions or provide any explanations pertaining to Nancy's disappearance.[ix] When first watching his media statement, Brad appeared awkward and unnatural, which was very similar to how his friends and neighbors described him on the day of Nancy's disappearance. He looked like he was holding something back. Was he hiding something? Upon closer review, Brad appeared very sad. He had to hold back his emotions, which was something very unusual for him. Brad was soft-spoken and unsure of himself. He was not used to giving public statements. Everyone wanted to know why the husband of the missing woman had not spoken publicly. The clear implication was that he was guilty. Of what, we did not know at the time. Neither the media nor the public adhere to the presumption of innocent until proven guilty.

Chapter 4 – From Missing Person to Homicide

Around 4:30 p.m. on July 14, 2008, William Lee Boyer took his dog for a walk in his neighborhood, The Oaks at Meadow Ridge. The Oaks is located on the outskirts of Cary, near Holly Springs Road, which is a busy two-lane road. At the end of a wooded cul-de-sac Mr. Boyer came upon the body of a female lying face down in a drainage ditch. She was naked, except for a sports bra. At the time, the area where he discovered the body was in the process of being developed, but it was fairly isolated. He found the unidentified body just off an unnamed road near Fielding Drive, a few miles from the Cooper home. The road has since been named Brittabby Court. Mr. Boyer walked to the nearest house and called the police.[lxi]

The body was not initially identified. However, there are very few dead bodies found in the town of Cary. As a result, the police immediately suspected it was Nancy. Utilizing dental records, the medical examiner identified the body as that of Nancy Cooper. He later ruled the death a homicide, and determined the cause of death as most likely asphyxia by strangulation.

The police who first arrived on the scene likely considered homicide probable, and the area was treated as a crime scene. The surrounding area was cordoned off, access was restricted, and evidence was collected. Though there were tire tracks, foot prints, and a cigarette butt found near Nancy's body, the police seemed skeptical as to whether the items were connected to her death. The police photographed and measured the tire tracks, but failed to cast them. Due to the standing water in the tire marks, the police were unable to determine the tread.[lxii] The police measured the distance between the two parallel tire tracks. They compared this measurement against both of the Cooper's cars and neither matched. The Cooper's cars both had measurements that were larger than what the police identified at the crime scene.[lxiii]

While searching the crime scene, the police found footprints in the mud very close to Nancy's body. The prints were filled with water, which prevented the police from casting them. They measured the footprints, and they did not match Brad's shoe size. According to the man who discovered the body, he did not leave any footprints, as he never left the asphalt on the nearby road.[lxiv] The footprints were a legitimate connection to the killer, yet the police did not go to great lengths to preserve and capture what could have been critical forensic evidence. Both the tire tracks and footprints were filled with water, but based on the likely evidentiary value, why was more effort not focused on capturing and collecting as detailed information as possible?

The police collected a cigarette butt near the body, but did not immediately send it to the North Carolina State Bureau of Investigation (SBI) for analysis. The police claimed they could not initially send all collected evidence to the SBI because it would overwhelm the organization. They only initially sent what they thought was the most critical evidence.[lxv] The police determined that a cigarette butt was not highly relevant evidence, even though it was found close to Nancy's body. Had the police already zeroed in on Brad and knew he did not smoke? The police may not have known where Nancy was killed, but they knew the killer had been where Nancy's body was found. Initially insignificant items could turn out to be the sole link between the crime scene and a suspect. Everything should have been collected and analyzed. Other items were collected from the crime scene and were either not analyzed for years or not properly preserved. The crime scene investigation lacked an appreciation for detail. Interestingly, nothing pulled from the crime scene implicated Brad in Nancy's death. As would become a common trait of this investigation, when evidence failed to implicate Brad, the police failed to investigate thoroughly. While Nancy was still a missing person, Cary Police Chief Pat Bazemore characterized Nancy's disappearance as an isolated incident insinuating that the culprit was likely someone close to Nancy. During a news conference on July 14, Chief Bazemore felt the need to correct media reports when they stated that Brad was the one who reported Nancy missing, but she refused to correct the media when they asked if Brad had purchased bleach on the morning of Nancy's disappearance.[lxvi] Interestingly, Chief Bazemore chose to correct information that showed Brad in a favorable manner, but not correct information that cast Brad in a guilty light.

Had detectives already informed Chief Bazemore that they had their sights set on Brad? Were they already ruling out other potential options? At the time of this press conference, the police had not spoken to numerous witnesses who claimed to have seen Nancy running on the morning she went missing. Did Chief Bazemore know something no one else knew or was she merely assuring the public everyone was safe, regardless of the facts? Now, her subordinates had to either deliver on her statement (promise) of an *isolated incident* or allow her to look bad in public.

The police were showing their hand. They believed someone close to Nancy had killed her. And based on the repeated questions and singular focus on Brad, it was fairly clear who they thought had done it. Many of Brad's initial statements were not consistent with what their other sources (Nancy's friends) were telling them. Further, things he told the police contradicted their observations, such as Brad's claim that he had recently cleaned yet the house was a complete mess when they arrived on the afternoon of July 12.

Once the police decided Brad lied to them, he was guilty in their eyes. Instincts are critical to an investigator, but so is objectivity. As the police pieced together clues and evidence, they devised a theory as to how and why Brad killed his wife, Nancy Cooper, and the manner in which he covered up the crime.

The police theorized that Nancy arrived home shortly after midnight on the evening of July 11 / morning of July 12, 2008. She had been drinking. Nancy and Brad had been fighting all day about money. Nancy embarrassed Brad a few hours earlier at the neighbor's cookout. She chastised him in front of friends and neighbors. Brad was livid at the way Nancy had treated him. He waited for her to come home. He wanted to let Nancy know how upset he was at the way she treated him at the party.

As Nancy walked in the front door, Brad immediately started yelling at her. Nancy yelled back, only fueling the fire already brewing within him. The argument escalated, and Brad got in Nancy's face. Nancy felt threatened for the first time in their marriage. She pushed Brad back, knocking over items in the foyer. The years of holding in his emotions and anger boiled to the surface. He had never thought about hurting her. But now it did not matter. He was enraged. Brad grabbed Nancy around the throat and did not let go until she was dead. She was barely able to put up a fight as he totally caught her by surprise. As he strangled her, she vomited the contents of her stomach all over her dress. He let her lifeless body drop to the foyer floor.

He lost his temper for the first time in his life, and Brad did not have a plan for what to do next. He was suddenly aware of his girls upstairs, and he wanted to make sure neither one of them saw their mother lying dead. For one, it would likely cause significant emotional trauma which would plague them the rest of their lives. Another, they would become witnesses to their mother's murder. As a result, Brad dragged Nancy's lifeless body into the kitchen. He needed to find a way to get the body out of the house. Otherwise, he would have to create an entirely fake crime scene in the house. He also had to get rid of any evidence linking him to Nancy's death.

Since Nancy had vomited, Brad removed Nancy's dress. He also removed everything Nancy was wearing, except for her earrings. Brad put her underwear, bra, and flip flops into a garbage bag for later removal. As he slowly started to concoct a cover story, he proceeded upstairs. He threw her dress, which contained the most incriminating evidence, into a laundry bin in the master bedroom, figuring no one would look for the dress she wore the previous night. Brad decided he would claim Nancy went running in the morning and never came back. Therefore, he would need to dress her in running clothes and set the stage for a run later in the morning. He returned to the kitchen from upstairs, but with only a sports bra. He decided to only have her wear a sports bra, maybe to make it look like a sexual attack. Nancy's lifeless body was lying nude on the kitchen floor. Brad tried to put the sports bra on her, but it was too tight. He was only able to pull it over her arms and shoulders. He gave up and left it there.

Next, Brad wanted to put Nancy's body into the trunk of his car, which would allow him to dispose of it in a secluded location. Though it was pitch dark in the middle of the night, Brad opted for moving the car into the garage rather than carrying Nancy's body out to his car in the driveway. There was one huge problem: the garage was packed with toys and boxes. He needed to clean the garage. To facilitate this endeavor, Brad had to hide the body. He could not leave his children's dead, naked mother lying on the kitchen floor where they could uncover it. He proceeded to drag Nancy's body into the small bathroom on the first floor. He positioned the body against the door in order to prevent the girls from opening it.

After successfully hiding the body, Brad returned to the garage. The garage was a complete mess. There was no possible way to fit a car in the garage. It did not matter; Brad needed to put his car in the garage to facilitate the transfer of Nancy's body into the trunk. With a murder having been recently committed and the evidence of such only a few feet away, Brad proceeded to spend hours cleaning the right side of the garage. All of the toys and clutter were placed on top of all the items and boxes on the other side of the garage.

Once clean, Brad pulled his car into the garage. He found a plastic drop cloth in the garage, which he used to completely cover the interior of his trunk. The drop cloth was brand new, which would ensure it would not transfer anything to Nancy's body. Brad returned to the first floor bathroom. He carried Nancy's dead body to his car and dropped her in the trunk. He then opened the garage door for the second time and backed the car onto the driveway. Brad left Nancy's lifeless body in the trunk and returned to the garage. He shut the garage door and then proceeded to mop the garage floor. He had to ensure he did not leave any evidence from when he carried her body through the garage.

After mopping the garage, Brad went back inside to clean the house. He needed to eliminate any evidence of Nancy's death. After cleaning for several more hours, Brad drove, with Nancy's body in the trunk, to Harris Teeter to establish an alibi. He left the girls alone at home. Upon arriving back at the house, he arranged for a remote call to come into his cell phone from the home line on his way to Harris Teeter for a second trip. During his second trip without the girls, Brad dumped Nancy's body at the end of a wooded cul-de-sac off of Fielding Drive, a few miles from the Cooper residence. After dumping her body and changing his shoes, Brad received the *fake*, remote call, thus validating that Nancy was still alive at 6:40 a.m.

After Brad returned home from the second Harris Teeter trip, he continued to clean the house and wait for someone to report Nancy missing. Prior to conducting additional cleaning, he perused the Internet for hours looking up such items as power-washing the house and hours of operation for a local museum. He pretended to look for Nancy during the afternoon and then returned home when the police arrived. For the next two days he operated a campaign of misinformation to confuse and misdirect the police. Or so the police believed.

Though it was very early in the investigation, unless some overwhelming evidence could be brought forward proving Brad's innocence, the only thing left for the police to do was collect the information necessary to support an arrest warrant. As they began this process, the police came across two items which significantly impaired their theory regarding Brad's guilt. A phone call was made from the Cooper residence to Brad's cell phone at 6:40 a.m. on the morning of July 12, and 16 eyewitnesses came forward stating they saw someone who looked like Nancy running on the morning of her disappearance. The phone call early in the morning would indicate to most people that Nancy was still alive. And numerous eyewitnesses claiming to have seen Nancy running would also indicate she was still alive on the morning of July 12. Rather than step back and determine what this new information meant, the police immediately set out to discredit the evidence.

Confirmation of a call from the Cooper home phone to Brad's cell at a time when the police theorized Nancy was dead posed a significant problem. There had to be another explanation, since their theory concluded Nancy was dead hours before the call was made. The first angle the police pursued involved someone assisting Brad by making the call for him. The police pulled Brad's friend, Mike Hiller, into the police station for questioning. During the interrogation the police tried to get Mike to admit he made the 6:40 a.m.

from the Cooper's residence.[lxvii] Mike did not crumble. He denied the police's claims. The police hit a wall and had to find another way the call could have been made.

With Brad's expertise with Internet phones, the police pursued the possibility Brad may have triggered the call remotely. They postulated that he spoofed a call to try to prove Nancy was still alive prior to her morning run. To the police their theory was more than a mere hypothesis; much like the psychic powers of Nancy's friends and neighbors, the police just *knew* Brad killed Nancy. He killed her in the home after she returned from the party. As a result, Nancy could not have called Brad at 6:40 a.m. during his second trip to Harris Teeter.

On the morning of July 12, video tape from the Harris Teeter grocery store surveillance cameras show Brad entered the store at 6:42 a.m. during his second trip.[lxviii] Since the Cooper residence was no more than two minutes away from the Harris Teeter store and Nancy was supposedly dead at this time, there had to be another answer as Brad could not have made the call himself. Mike Hiller denied making the call. After several dead ends, the police concluded that Brad remotely triggered the call using sophisticated telephone equipment from his workplace, Cisco Systems. Brad had significant expertise in the voice-over-Internet-protocol arena. Brad was capable of triggering a remote call. Further, Cisco produced equipment capable of remotely initiating a telephone call. It was possible.

The theory had one slight problem: there was no evidence supporting their conclusion. The police could not find any equipment in the Cooper residence capable of initiating a remote call. There was no evidence found of a remotely initiated call on Cisco's call logs. No one saw Brad initiate the remote call. The theory was supported by nothing other than backing into it by assuming a conclusion where a remotely initiated call must have happened.

Though the police likely zeroed in on Brad early in the investigation, the discovery of the 6:40 a.m. phone call should have given them a compelling reason to rethink their prime "person of interest." This should have been a huge red flag to the police. Brad may not have been their guy. Unfortunately, rather than cause the police to rethink their theory, it somehow hardened their convictions in Brad's guilt.

The police had a much easier approach to the problem of 16 eyewitnesses who claimed to have seen Nancy jogging on the morning of July 12, 2008.[lxix] They must all be mistaken. The witnesses saw someone who looked like Nancy, but it was not Nancy. It could not have been Nancy; she was already dead. As a result, 16 eyewitnesses were essentially dismissed, even though some of them had yet to be interviewed.

The police failed to thoroughly investigate the death of Nancy Cooper. Their focus was on Brad. As Jessica Adam led the charge, the police followed right along. The Cary Police Department interviewed Brad several times on the day of Nancy's disappearance as well as subsequent days. Many of Brad's responses lead the police to believe Brad was lying to them. And police equate lying with guilt. Brad lied about cleaning the house. Brad said he cleaned an area, but it did not look clean. Brad claimed that he did laundry, but Nancy's friends stated that he never did laundry.

Many of the areas where the police believed Brad lied were very subjective areas. How is your marriage? Do you help around the house? How often does Nancy go jogging? Each one of these questions could garner completely different answers depending on the interviewer and how the questions were asked. In the 1977 Oscar-winning movie *Annie Hall*, Woody Allen's character and Diane Keaton's character were dating, but experiencing some relationship problems. There was an arrangement where the director bounced back and forth between scenes where each character was asked the same question: "How often do you have sex?" Woody Allen's character responded, "Never, we probably only have sex three times a week." The scene then flashes to Diane Keaton's character where she responded, "All the time, probably three times a week."

Was one of the characters lying or did they merely have different perspectives on the same situation? Obviously, it was the latter. Brad told the police he and Nancy were having marital problems. He told the police they slept in separate bedrooms and even mentioned his affair. Notwithstanding, Brad also conveyed to the police that he thought their relationship was getting better and things were normal for them. The police viewed this as a lie, since Nancy's family and friends told them divorce was imminent. Was Brad lying or was this a difference of opinion? With regard to Brad, the police took differences of opinion and equated it with deception.

Another error the police made was having numerous people ask Brad very similar questions. Depending on the question, one could get different variations of the same answer. The police did not record the questions or the answers for comparison purposes. They were merely discussing the interactions among themselves. For example, one detective stated Brad said he cleaned the foyer and hallway and another detective stated, "But he told me he also cleaned the bathroom in the hall." As a result, the detectives thought Brad was lying about what he cleaned because their answers were not exactly in line. There are numerous flaws with this methodology, though granted, there were likely many times where this approach worked well.

Each detective likely asked Brad slightly different questions, which undoubtedly affected his responses. One may have asked an open-ended question, such as, "What rooms of the house did you clean?" Another detective may have asked specific questions, such as, "Did you clean the kitchen? Did you clean the hall bathroom?" The format of the question alone could result in different answers, which did not take into account that Brad may have remembered more the second or third time he was asked similar questions. We also know Brad was under tremendous stress during the time he was questioned, and many of the questions probably seemed completely unimportant to him. Another factor in the questioning could have been time frame. What if one detective asked him what he cleaned during the morning while a different detective asked what he cleaned during the day? If Brad cleaned an area after noon, he may have rightfully excluded the area from his answer regarding cleaning during the morning, thus providing an accurate answer yet different from his other response.

If Brad were trying to deceive the detectives, their approach would not have likely uncovered the deception. The detective's approach was too inconsistent and inaccurate. Brad's inability to connect with people socially and emotionally was likely working against him with the police now. Social awkwardness can make people feel uncomfortable. When someone feels uncomfortable, they want to extract themselves from the situation. And it usually results in negative feelings toward the person creating the uncomfortable situation, and often times this does not happen on the conscious level. Brad's odd demeanor and poor social skills likely made him unlikable to the police. In general, people are much less tolerant of people they do not like than those they do. As a result, everything begins to build on the previous item. Brad acted strangely. He was uncomfortable talking to the police and then his answers seemed off. Rather than stepping back and assessing the situation objectively, the police likely put their gut feelings together and saw a problem. Brad was being deceptive, and deception usually means guilt.

One police officer also noted that golf was on the television when he arrived at the Cooper residence on the twelfth of July. He did not think it made sense in light of the nature of the call to the police.[lxx] The described scene implied that Brad was relaxed at home watching golf when his wife was missing. Let us assume Brad brutally murdered Nancy less than 15 hours earlier. Under this scenario, how could Brad possibly be relaxed? The implied assumption was that Brad is a psychopath, completely unaffected by other's pain and suffering. For a lay person, who receives his information on crime from television dramas, it may have been a reasonable conclusion. However, this was a police detective. He should not have been so easily drawn to an uninformed, inexperienced conclusion.

If Brad did kill Nancy, he would have most likely been completely fearful of getting caught, but trying to appear concerned. Watching golf does not fit into a rage murder. Brad had not been accused of killing numerous other people. He was not an alleged serial killer. He was merely a potential witness at that time. The police did not even know who turned on the television, or if it was on for the girls earlier in the day, and then golf came on the same station. The police were making poor assumptions, which adversely affected the scope and breadth of the investigation.

Later, when the police reviewed the video tapes of Brad at Harris Teeter on the morning of July 12, they found it odd he was wearing a long-sleeve shirt and long pants.[lxxi] It was the middle of July in North Carolina. He must have been hiding something, even though Brad wore shorts and a short-sleeved shirt later in the day. Who would wear long-sleeves and pants during the worst heat of the summer? The high on July 12, 2008 was 89 degrees Fahrenheit in Cary, but it was only around 68 degrees at the time Brad visited the grocery store.[lxxii] It was uncommon for someone to where long-sleeves, but was it uncommon for Brad? Brad wore long-sleeves during the press conference he attended two days later and when he searched for Nancy on July 16, both hotter days than the twelfth.[lxxiii] Though Brad's wearing long-sleeves on other days should have served as vindication that it was not an unusual apparel choice for him, the police viewed it as additional manipulation by Brad.

As the homicide investigation kicked into full gear, the Cary Police Department began making some questionable decisions on which leads to follow and which ones to ignore, though the overall trend was very consistent: follow anything pointing toward Brad and discard items pointing away from him. On the afternoon of Nancy's disappearance, family friends Mike and Clea Morwick, watched the Cooper's two daughters. While at the Morwick's, the Cooper's older daughter, Bella, told Clea that she saw her mother wearing jogging clothes earlier that morning.[lxxiv] At the time, Bella was only four years old. Clea informed the police of Bella's comment, but the police chose not to interview her due to her age.

The police felt interviewing Bella would cause her undue stress and trauma.[lxxv] It was a plausible and reasonable explanation for why they chose not to interview her. However, the police interview young children all the time when the children are the victims of a crime. Sometimes they utilize child psychologists or other professionals, but the police still obtain the information. The Cary Police Department chose not to pursue the lead at all. According to Brad, Bella was asleep until after Nancy left for her run; therefore, the information she provided could have been useful to the investigation. Interestingly, it was likely another lead that would have been exculpatory to Brad.

At the location where Nancy's body was found, the police failed to capture many aspects of the crime scene. Though the police had legitimate reasons for not casting the tire tracks and foot prints, it was another example of questions left unanswered where additional effort may have generated very useful information

The police did not check Nancy's Facebook page for private messages.[lxxvi] Though it may have been taken slightly out of context, one Cary police officer told a witness that "consistency was good" when relaying stories about the Coopers.[lxxvii] The Cary Police Department was racking up numerous mistakes and errors in judgment. Though the police made many mistakes as a result of inexperience or poor decision-making, some of their actions appeared less accidental. Furthermore, most of the incompetence and lack of thoroughness involved areas which may have exonerated Brad.

An example of such incompetence occurred when Detective Jim Young of the Cary Police Department attempted to access Nancy's locked Blackberry phone. Detective Young did not have any specific training or expertise in the arena of data extraction from cellular devices. Regardless, he contacted an unknown person at AT&T who attempted to walk him through unlocking Nancy's phone. On August 9, 2008, Detective Young destroyed all the data stored on the phone by incorrectly entering the wrong passcode 10 times on two occasions, one round for the Subscriber Identification Module (SIM) card and another round for the phone itself.[lxxviii]

Prior to Detective Young's destruction of the cell phone, Brad's attorneys sent a certified letter to the Cary Police Department specifically requesting the police to take measures to protect the data on Nancy's Blackberry phone. The department received the letter on August 6, 2008. Detective Young destroyed all of the data specifically noted in the letter three days later.[lxxix] Detective Young did not document the steps he took when he attempted to access the phone. He later sought a search warrant for the contents of the phone, and he failed to mention the phone's data may have already been destroyed.[lxxx] At the request of lead Detective Gregory Daniels, Detective Young sent a letter to Brad's attorneys notifying them of the destruction of evidence within Nancy's phone. The letter was not sent until June of 2009, which was too late for Brad's attorneys or the police to recover the destroyed information.[lxxxi]

Nancy's phone may have contained texts, pictures, and other information relevant to the investigation into her murder. Unfortunately, we will never know since the evidence was destroyed. During a *Dateline* interview, assistant district attorney and prosecutor on this case, Howard Cummings, did not seem too concerned about the phone's destruction. He stated, "We already knew all of her friends."[lxxxii] Apparently, no one associated with this case felt the need to conduct a comprehensive investigation.

Was the phone's data destroyed inadvertently or intentionally? Detective Young had extensive experience within law enforcement. Police officers are generally considered unbiased within an investigation. He should not have had any motivation to sway the investigation one way or the other. Though he had extensive *general* law enforcement experience, Detective Young did not have any experience with extracting data from cellular phones. Mistakes do happen.

To the contrary, the defense's telephone expert, Ben Levitan, found many of Detective Young's actions when handling the phone to be highly suspect. For Detective Young to have erased the data, it required him to enter codes repeatedly into the phone. The phone provided warnings that indicated if he continued to enter incorrect codes data would be permanently erased. He disregarded the warnings and proceeded to delete the data anyway. Upon deleting the data, Detective Young failed to immediately notify anyone of the problem or take steps to try to regain the lost data. He simply returned the phone to inventory and proceeded to analyze other evidence. Detective Young also completely disregarded several police procedures involving the handling of digital evidence. Mr. Levitan found it highly implausible that Detective Young could have *accidently* deleted the phone's data in the manner which he claimed. He opined that Detective Young intentionally deleted the data on Nancy's Blackberry.[lxxxiii]

While the police were investigating Brad, Nancy's family, the Rentzs, moved to seek custody of Bella and Katie Cooper. They received emergency custody of the girls on July 16, 2008, the day after Nancy's body was identified. In a blink, Brad's daughters were taken from him. It was a harbinger of things to come.

For permanent custody, the process would be a little more drawn out. Though many of the affidavits submitted on behalf of Nancy's family tried to show that Brad was not a good father, it was merely a distraction from the real issue: the belief that Brad killed Nancy. As a warm-up for the criminal trial, the Rentzs provided rumors and hearsay as evidence of Brad's unfitness as a father. Brad worked long hours. He had an affair. He focused on himself. Nancy primarily took care of the children. All of these statements may have been true, but it was not clear how any of it had any bearing on Brad's ability to regain custody of his children. The Rentzs took regular and normal distribution of household duties by a couple and used it as justification for removing children from their father.

For all the evidence accumulated, there was nothing indicating Brad was an unfit father. Probably the most compelling *evidence* in support of Brad as a father was Nancy's statements. Though Nancy tended to exaggerate and garner sympathy for herself, she never stated Brad was an unfit father. According to Nancy, Brad did not spend enough time with the girls and then at other times he hovered too much; however, Nancy never said Brad was a bad father.

Further support for Brad's maintaining custody also came by way of Nancy in the separation agreement. As has been noted, Nancy asked for significant compensation in the separation agreement. The agreement essentially provided all assets and income to Nancy and all liabilities would remain with Brad. There was no attempt at concession or give-and-take. It was all take. Interestingly, Nancy did not seek sole custody. She provided for Brad to have significant visitation with the girls, though he did have to pay for all travel associated with the visits. If Nancy had any concerns about the safety of the girls, she would have stated her concerns in the separation agreement and sought to prevent Brad from seeing the girls without supervision. She did not.

In early October, 2008, Brad sat for a deposition regarding the custody of his girls. The deposition forced Brad to answer questions around the murder of Nancy, as nothing was considered off-limits. The deposition focused more on locking Brad into various answers regarding Nancy's death rather than gaining insights into his parenting competence. Brad took a huge risk by agreeing to the deposition. Clearly, Brad's potential loss of freedom did not deter him from trying to regain custody of his girls. A slight change or variation in anything he said would be viewed by the police as deception. The police had zeroed in on Brad, and he knew it. The deposition provided an opportunity for the police to find inconsistencies in his answers, no matter how subtle or unrelated to Nancy's death they may have been.

While the custody case was ongoing, the police were also at work. The issue hanging over the custody battle was the belief that Brad may have killed Nancy. There was an appearance of impropriety hovering over Brad. As the custody case was playing out, the police arrested Brad and charged him with murder. The courts gave the Rentz's temporary custody of Bella and Katie on November 21, 2008, and they were later awarded full custody since Brad's incarceration prevented him from caring for his children.[lxxxiv]

Chapter 5 – From Investigation to Prosecution

"It's all a circus. A three ring circus. This trial...the whole world. It's all...show business." - *Chicago*

Shortly after Brad gave his deposition for the custody case, the police got the break they needed. The FBI found evidence on Brad's work computer of a Google Maps search of the exact area where Nancy's body was found. The search took place on the eleventh of July, the day before Nancy went missing. As a result, Brad was indicted for murder on October 27, 2008.[lxxxv] The case against Brad Cooper shifted from the police to the Wake County District Attorney's Office.

The prosecutors assigned to the case were three assistant district attorneys from Wake County: Howard J. Cummings, Boz Zellinger, and Amy Fitzhugh. Brad was defended by local attorneys, Howard Kurtz and Robert Trenkle. The trial was presided over by Judge Paul Gesner, a former police officer and prosecutor. The wheels of justice moved slowly and years passed before the trial began. It did not start until February 28, 2011, almost two and a half years later. The trial was one of the longest in Wake County history. It lasted 10 weeks, with the prosecution's case taking up the majority of the time. The State's witness list looked like a shortened version of the phone book. Anyone who may have known, spoken to, or heard of Nancy or Brad Cooper was pulled into court to testify. It was an extremely long court case, yet there was minimal evidence presented. At one point, the jury sent a note to the judge asking to speed the trial along.[lxxxvi] They wanted to get on with their lives.

A trial allows each side to present evidence. Trials are supposed to be won or lost on what can be proven. The State of North Carolina versus Bradley Cooper was not rooted in evidence nor did the trial attempt to seek the truth. When it comes to actually understanding what happened to Nancy Cooper, the 2011 trial was primarily noise. Facts were hard to find. How could a case with essentially one piece of evidence last 10 weeks? The prosecution was about to demonstrate just how to do that.

Prior to a criminal trial, the prosecution is required to turn over *all* information and evidence that it intends to use against the defendant during the trial.[lxxxvii] This period is called "discovery." Discovery is intended to provide the defendant with the opportunity to review all evidence against him. It affords him the opportunity of a fair and reasonable defense. Further, by the prosecution's providing the defendant all the evidence upfront, a defendant may be more likely to negotiate a plea, thus avoiding the burden and cost of a trial.[lxxxviii] As part of discovery, the defense is also required to turn over various pieces of information to the prosecution, but it is a less comprehensive burden. Overall, the discovery period is designed to provide a level of fairness to the defendant whereby he is entitled to any information that could be exculpatory (i.e., information that may cause a reasonable person to doubt the guilt of the accused).[lxxxix]

As discovery began, the defense encountered significant issues in trying to obtain information from the State. The prosecutors seemed to be playing a game with the defense. They withheld information because of technicalities, claimed they already provided it, and at times, failed to even give an answer for not providing requested information. Were the prosecutors not acting in good faith? According to the American Bar Association (ABA),

- A prosecutor should not intentionally fail to make timely disclosure to the defense, at the earliest feasible opportunity, of the existence of all evidence or information which tends to negate the guilt of the accused or mitigate the offense charged or which would tend to reduce the punishment of the accused.
- A prosecutor should not fail to make a reasonably diligent effort to comply with a legally proper discovery request.[xc]

Apparently, the Wake County prosecutors had a different interpretation of the ABA's standards. The defense team was forced to compel discovery three times during the fall of 2008 alone. Though some of the information in the State's case was evolving, gaps existed and information was omitted on many of the submissions to the defense. The two sides continued to bicker over discovery, with the State withholding as much as they could. On December 5, 2008, the court ordered the prosecution to provide discovery within 90 days. Shortly after the order, the prosecution provided 1,000 pages of discovery to the defense.[xci]

After a discovery compliance hearing in February of 2009, the prosecution turned over another 3,000 pages as part of discovery.[xcii] Though the amount of discoverable items turned over to the defense was massive, the State failed to turn over several evidentiary and potentially exculpatory items. Rather than facilitating a fair and appropriate judicial process, the State seemed to have little concern for the rights of the accused. Let the defense worry about that. The only justice the prosecutors appeared to be concerned with was a conviction. They felt no obligation to provide what is usual and customary prior to a criminal trial.

Over the next year, the battle for discovery continued. The defense was continually forced to utilize the courts to get the State to fulfill their obligations under discovery. In March of 2010, the defense again went back to court to compel the State to provide what they believed were discoverable items. The court required the State to provide some of the requested items, but many of the requested items were denied. The court refused to compel the prosecution to turn over information regarding whether or not the Cooper daughter, Bella, had been interviewed by the police. The court found that the information was not discoverable as it could be covered on cross-examination; however, during the trial the court prevented the defense from asking anyone questions regarding the decision not to interview Bella.

The court also denied the defense's requests for information the police had developed pertaining to any of Nancy's potential sexual relationships, details on her social media activities, and any information the Rentz's attorney, Alice Stubbs, provided to the police. The court also denied the request for any information pertaining to a specific detective's experience and training, even though detectives routinely provide this information when requesting warrants.[xciii] Many of the denied requests were potentially exculpatory, but the most troubling denial pertained to the role of the FBI.

The Cary Police Department utilized the FBI's Computer Analysis Response Team (CART) to review and analyze many of the computers, hard drives, and other technological equipment seized from the Coopers' home and Cisco's offices. During the FBI's review of one of Brad's computers, it found evidence of a Google Maps search of Fielding Drive, specifically where Nancy's body was found. Based on the extracted information, the search was conducted on the afternoon before Nancy went missing. The Google Maps evidence was the primary basis for the arrest warrant of Brad Cooper.

The judge denied the defense's request for copies of the FBI's policies and procedures on the basis of national security. Understandably, the FBI evaluates computers in cases involving international terrorists, espionage, and drug-trafficking to name a few. The FBI must protect its methodologies and procedures from persons who could potentially harm the United States. Certain materials and information are classified for good reasons. The need to protect the country, in certain circumstances, outweighs the right to have access to specific, limited information. However, the case against Brad Cooper did not involve national security. It was not even a federal offense.

The judge denied the defense's request for the FBI CART policies and procedures. The judge could have reviewed the questioned items in chambers (also, referred to as "in camera"). The secondary action would have allowed the judge to review the requested items more thoroughly while outside of the public's view. He could have determined if certain portions of the policies and procedures could have been admitted rather than provide a blanket denial. In addition, if the defense appealed the discovery decision, the Court of Appeals would have a basis for review.[xciv]

By allowing all of the information involved in how the FBI arrived at its conclusions to be outside the scope of discovery, it materially impacted Brad's ability to sufficiently defend himself. If the FBI's methodologies cannot be released to a defendant, then the FBI should not be utilized, except under very rare and compelling circumstances. Otherwise, defendants, and society as a whole, will just have to trust that State witnesses did not make a mistake or intentionally alter the results. One side would be allowed to operate under the honor system while the other side is held to a higher standard. The judge opened the door for law enforcement agencies to utilize the FBI as a means to avoid discovery. Their conclusions would become almost unimpeachable. Brad's defense team was left with limited ability to refute the State's expert witnesses on the most critical piece of evidence against Brad. Heading into trial, the defense team knew it would be an uphill battle as the playing field was far from level.

The police demonstrated an inability to lift their focus off of Brad. Facts directly contrary to their theory did not persuade them to look at other suspects or even question their beliefs. Certainly, with the case shifting to the Wake County District Attorney's Office, the experienced prosecutors would question and challenge any and all the inconsistencies in the police's case. They are separate from the police. They serve as a legal control on overzealous police departments. Additionally, they are intelligent, knowledgeable lawyers. They do not have a bias toward believing everything the police told them. Their job is to question the assumptions and conclusions presented by the police.

The prosecution failed to ensure justice. There was a clear absence of critical thinking by the Wake County prosecutors in this case. The prosecutors appeared to spend more time rationalizing inconsistencies than evaluating flawed and conflicting information provided by the police. Why were the prosecutors not asking the police tough questions? Why were they not digging into the assumptions being made? If Brad were black and the prosecutors were white, one could have claimed racism. If Brad were female and all of the prosecutors were male, one could have claimed sexism. However, there was no clear reason for why the police, and now the prosecutors, appeared to disregard logic and their sworn duties in pursuing Brad Cooper. The primary factor behind the police's actions appeared to be incompetence. The Cary Police Department rarely encountered murders. In the five years prior to 2008, there were only three murders in Cary.[xcv] Nonetheless, the Wake County prosecutors did not have this excuse. Homicides regularly occur in Wake County.

Prosecutors work closely with local police departments. As a result, the prosecutors get to know the police officers and trust them. When a trusted officer explains a case to them, they tend to believe the officer. The police officer usually paints the accused as a less than stellar pillar of society, which is an accurate depiction most of the time. Allegations of false accusations and police fabrications or tampering of evidence are looked at skeptically. They are viewed as attempts to divert the attention away from the crime the accused has allegedly committed.

Talk to defense attorneys and the conversation is much different. They will tell you stories of clients who have been falsely accused of child abuse by an angry ex-spouse. Situations where clients were arrested by a police officer who lied about the facts of the case. There are countless stories of injustice. Interestingly, there are many defense attorneys who were former prosecutors. They have seen both sides of cases, yet sympathize with victims of the justice system.

Who has the most accurate depiction of criminal cases? In short, they both do. Generally, the prosecutors are correct, but they do not account for the outliers. They fail to recognize cases where those in authority abuse their positions. Unfortunately, there are also times when victims fabricate charges. The accused faces a huge uphill battle trying to prove his/her innocence. On the other side, defense attorneys remember the rare instance where they had an innocent client who was the victim of law enforcement malfeasance.

The prosecutors in Brad's case seemed to be held hostage by their experience as well. Experience provides a tremendous base for evaluating current issues; however, it can also be quite detrimental. In the book, *The Black Swan* by Nassim Taleb, he describes a scenario with a farmer and a chicken. Each day the farmer feeds the chicken. Years pass, and every day that the farmer feeds the chicken, the chicken becomes less fearful of the farmer. Finally, the day arrives

when the farmer cuts the head off of the chicken.[xcvi]
Experience is not always an asset. At times, our experiences
cloud our understanding of our current situation.

It was not clear how much of the prosecution's actions fell
under the idea that the *ends justify the means* and how much
was a result of their comfort with bending the law and
professional standards as far as they could within a given
situation or trial. The prosecutors chose to present non-
evidentiary information throughout the trial. They allowed
and enabled witnesses to present half-truths in court.
According to the ABA, a prosecutor's duty goes beyond
receiving a conviction; he is supposed to seek justice.[xcvii]

The 2011 trial dragged on for months. The State wasted a
tremendous amount of time presenting rumors and gossip.
Most of the State's case focused on hearsay. It was geared
toward conveying various themes and narratives rather than
presenting evidence. The themes focused on the concept
that Brad was a bad guy. He did not provide for his wife
and children. He was cold. He was controlling and a work-
a-holic. Brad was self-centered. Further, during their
divorce, Brad and Nancy were angry with each other.
Weeks and weeks of the State's case were geared towards
proving these items. They were points that could not be
proven because of their subjective nature. And even if they
could have been proven, they had nothing to do with
Nancy's murder. The ABA standards specifically state, "The
prosecutor should not make arguments calculated to appeal
to the prejudices of the jury."[xcviii] Generally, character
evidence is viewed as providing little evidentiary value, and
it is considered highly prejudicial. Character evidence is
deemed more to reward good behavior and punish bad

behavior rather than to allow the jury to focus on the facts of the case at hand.[xcix] It is hard to rationalize how presenting the above information throughout the trial was not designed specifically to appeal to the prejudices of the jury. It had nothing to do with Nancy's murder.

One circumstance within the case that should have given the prosecutors reason to pause was the phone call from the Cooper residence to Brad's cell phone at 6:40 a.m. on the morning of July 12. Their theory hinged on the fact that Nancy was dead hours before this call. If so, who made the phone call? The prosecution got creative. They postulated that with Brad's telephone expertise, he must have remotely triggered the call using sophisticated equipment from his workplace. Because the call directly contradicted the State's theory, they had to address it. However, the prosecutors had no evidence of a remotely triggered call, and they knew it. As one of the prosecutors, Boz Zellinger stated on *Dateline*, "He [Brad] had the potential."[c] And potential was all they had.

The worst part of the State's theory of a remotely triggered call was its illogic nature. There was no need to remotely initiate a call. One did not need to be a voice-over-Internet-protocol (VOIP) expert to emulate a call from the home. Under the theory, Brad needed to make people believe Nancy was still alive. He also wanted to provide himself with an alibi, thus the two trips to the grocery store. Why would Brad go to the great lengths of creating and initiating a remote call to his cell when he could have just picked up the home phone and called his cell phone? Initiating a remote call would require time. It provided an electronic record. There would be evidence of the call. What possible reason could Brad have concocted to explain the remote call if and when it was discovered? It posed incredible risk with minimal upside benefit.

Any lay person who wanted to spoof a call from his spouse would have simply used the home phone to call his cell phone. The grocery store was only five minutes away; therefore, the received call would have been within five minutes of arrival at the store. One could have easily stated he received the call as he backed out of the driveway or just left the house. The police could have postulated that Brad made the call himself, but there would have been no proof. It was a much simpler solution.

Unfortunately for the prosecution, Brad received the call too close to when he arrived at the grocery store (as verified by the video tape). Brad could not have called himself. There was no reason why Brad would have gone to such sophisticated lengths to do something he could have done with rudimentary skills.

During the trial, the prosecution presented information alluding to the presence of a router capable of remotely initiating a call in the Cooper household. They interviewed people from Cisco who identified a missing router. They showed a misleading picture of a dusty shelf with a clear square area representing where the router could have been in the Cooper house. However, the picture was not even from Brad's desk.[ci]

The prosecutors demonstrated Brad was *capable* of remotely initiating a call. Nevertheless, there was no evidence an actual remotely-initiated call was made. Nor was there any information indicating Brad triggered the call. Further, there was no link between the router and Nancy's murder. The prosecution conveyed pure speculation about a missing router as if it were fact.

A trial is where arguments are presented and countered. It is supposed to be an intellectual exercise where the merits of a case are debated and dissected. However, in the Cooper trial there was very little actual evidence presented. Much of the trial focused on establishing an environment where gossip and hearsay provided the foundation for opinion. The themes and concepts covered a vast array of topics, and none of them, even if they could have been proven, provided any real information pertaining to the guilt or innocence of Brad. The State's primary themes included, among others: Brad controlled Nancy, the couple argued, Brad acted strangely on the day of Nancy's disappearance, Brad had an affair, Brad did not clean the house, and Nancy always wore her necklace.

How did the judge allow any of this information into court? It is hard to imagine a clear link between what was presented and its relevance. The jury had to connect what the prosecutors were presenting via witnesses to some other aspect of their theory, which tied to some other component of the case that was supposed to indirectly implicate Brad in Nancy's murder. Conclusively proving what the prosecutors presented would have potentially met the lowest level of circumstantial evidence. Regardless, how did the judge determine the probative value of the evidence outweighed the prejudicial aspects of it? The prosecutors claimed that since Brad did or did not do certain activities prior to the crime, it meant he was more or less likely to have conducted the alleged crime. It is similar to the debate over whether or not the prosecution can present evidence of previous convictions. Usually, previous offenses or behavior does not prove the defendant did *this* crime, and the introduction of this evidence is highly prejudicial. However, in this case, the judge felt the introduction of exhaustive, detailed alleged aspects of Brad's behaviors and mannerism were more compelling than the potential prejudice it inflicted upon the jury.

The determination of evidence admissibility was almost completely absent throughout the trial. It was hard to determine why certain witnesses were called and how their testimony related in any manner to Brad's guilt. At one point during the trial, the prosecution had Thomas Como from the City-County Bureau of Identification testify regarding evidence processed from the Cooper residence. He testified to streaks found on the garage floor and red spots on bed sheets. However, he indicated all areas were tested and no blood was found. As a local news story relayed it, "Prosecutors, however, haven't said how the evidence could be relevant to the case."[cii] As with most aspects of the prosecution's case, we were left without understanding how the evidence they presented had anything to do with the charges against Brad.

As they pushed their key themes, the prosecution attempted to lay the groundwork for the theory that Brad controlled Nancy. Unfortunately for them, there was no history of domestic violence. There was no evidence of *any* violence in their relationship. Because reality did not line up with the narrative, the State chose to focus on financial control. The

State then contended that financial control equated to domestic violence, though a budget was a far cry from physical violence. From there, the jury needed to draw the conclusion that domestic violence meant Brad was guilty. Brad allegedly controlled Nancy by putting her on a weekly cash budget of $300 for the last few months of her life. During a *Dateline* episode about Nancy's murder, the reporter was confused by the allegations of control. The following exchange took place:

Reporter: How do you tell a jury he [Brad] is depriving her [Nancy]?

Boz Zellinger: There are signs of control emanating from the Cooper household.

Howard Cummings: It doesn't matter whether it was $1,000 a week or $10 a week. The fact of the matter is that it caused friction between the two of them.[ciii]

Apparently, it did not matter what Brad did because if it caused friction, it was evidence of murder. He also did not allow her to have any credit cards or access to the bank accounts during this timeframe. The budget was instituted for very prudent reasons; Nancy's inability to control her spending was bankrupting the family and putting their financial future into grave jeopardy. Nancy's spending pushed the family closer and closer to bankruptcy, even though their income was well above average. Nancy was not responsible enough to be trusted with credit cards or access to the bank accounts. Nevertheless, prior to the budgetary constraints placed on Nancy in early 2008, she did whatever she wanted, whenever she wanted. And the budget only constricted her financially.

According to the State's own witness, Diana Duncan, Nancy spent every day at the pool during the summer. Countless other witnesses for the State testified to Nancy's numerous vacations, nights out with friends, and extra-curricular activities ad nauseam. Brad watched the girls in the evenings, which allowed Nancy to have fun with her friends, exercise, or do whatever she chose to do. With the budget, Nancy was only limited because she could only spend a finite amount of money each week on entertainment.

Several of the State's witnesses testified that they asked Nancy point blank if she was afraid of Brad and she said, "No." Nancy manipulated her friends as best she could with regard to her financial situation. She garnered tremendous sympathy without anyone questioning it. No one asked Nancy why a budget was necessary. No one asked if the family was having financial problems. Nancy blamed it on Brad's controlling nature and meanness. And though the State clearly knew the financial circumstances of the Coopers, they chose to push this angle in an attempt to garner the same sympathy Nancy achieved while she was alive. No evidence, no proof, and although the prosecutors knew it, yet they still pushed forward. The prosecutors were not concerned with evidence; this theme was designed to appeal to the prejudices of the jury. Furthermore, the conclusion they were trying to push the jury toward was at best tangential to the murder of Nancy Cooper. This entire portion of the trial lacked relevance.

On May 21, 2008, Jenipher Free, the parent of a child at Triangle Pre-school, which was where the Cooper girls attended, heard an argument in the parking lot. She was concerned enough to walk over and make sure everything was okay. She saw Brad and Nancy Cooper yelling at each other. Nancy was hysterical and crying. She yelled at Brad, "What are you trying to be, dad of the year?" Brad got into his car and sped off.[civ]

The prosecution had Ms. Free testify in order to help facilitate the theme that the Coopers argued. Jessica Adam, always helpful, stated that she once heard Brad raise his voice toward Nancy while she was on the phone with Nancy. Another witness for the State, Jennifer Fetterolf, testified that Nancy yelled at Brad while they were at her house in May of 2008. However, Brad did not respond to or engage with Nancy.

Brad and Nancy were married for almost 10 years. At the time of Nancy's death, they were in the process of separating, though still living together. The couple went to therapy together earlier in the year, and Nancy had a separation agreement drafted. Clearly, the couple was enduring serious problems. Anger was present. Arguments were expected. Yet, the prosecution tried to demonstrate that they argued as part of the murder trial. How was any of this relevant to the murder case? How did the judge allow this to be admitted as evidence?

Though *proving* Brad and Nancy argued did little to further the State's case, presenting information indicating the couple fought immediately prior to Nancy's disappearance was relevant. On July 11, Nancy was upset with Brad. She had

not received her weekly allowance from him. She told Diana
Duncan it was an "I hate Brad day!"[cv] Brad claimed he
forgot to give it to her, but at other times it seemed he may
have just decided she did not need an allowance for the
week since she received money from her parents while on
vacation. Either way, Nancy did not have her money.

When Brad arrived at the Duncan's house, Nancy let Brad
know exactly how she felt about his not providing her
allowance. Nancy clinched her fists and yelled at Brad, but
he did not respond. He appeared deflated and withdrawn
as Nancy chastised him. Several people stated it was the
first time they had seen the couple argue in public. Nancy
was clearly upset with Brad, but Brad did not demonstrate
any anger toward Nancy. Since Brad did not show any
outward signs of aggression, the State concluded he must
have felt humiliated and retaliated when Nancy got home
later in the evening. There was no evidence Brad felt
belittled, angry, or needed to get even with Nancy. It was
pure speculation. It was an all-to-common tactic; the State
utilized an absence of evidence as evidence. Brad did not
seem mad; therefore, he was mad, but did not display it.

Almost every State witness who saw Brad on the day Nancy
went missing was asked what they thought of Brad's
behaviors. The line of questioning was *poorly* designed to
elicit information regarding Brad's strangeness on July 12.
Apparently, the prosecution believed that there was
significant evidentiary value in how Brad acted in the face of
Nancy's disappearance. Numerous witnesses described
Brad's behavior as odd, rehearsed, unnatural, and false.
What did this mean? What did the prosecution want the
jury to think it meant?

Brad was under a tremendous amount of stress on the afternoon of July 12. His wife was missing. His friends and neighbors were openly expressing their belief he was involved in her disappearance. And the police were questioning him as if he were a suspect, or at least it appeared so to Brad. What was appropriate behavior versus inappropriate behavior under these circumstances? It was quite subjective, though by most accounts Brad acted strangely. However, to many people, Brad's regular demeanor was odd. When pushed, most witnesses acknowledged that Brad's demeanor on the day Nancy went missing was consistent with his general demeanor. Of course, this acknowledgement did not persuade them to think his behavior was any less suspicious.

And suspicious was exactly what the prosecution wanted the jury to be. They wanted the jury to conclude that Brad had acted suspiciously and guiltily. His behaviors were consistent with a murderer trying to cover his tracks rather than a concerned husband. However, most of Brad's behaviors and actions aligned with that of a concerned and stressed husband. Brad actively searched for Nancy. He called people trying to locate friends she may have been with. To the prosecutors, Brad's avoiding eye contact and remaining quiet was relevant evidence of his guilt.

During her court testimony, the Cooper's neighbor, Diana Duncan repeatedly laughed and giggled. Her neighbor was dead. Her other neighbor was being tried for murder, yet she chuckled throughout her testimony. Her laughter was definitely strange and inappropriate. Nonetheless, she was likely nervous, and some people laugh when they get nervous. Unfortunately, no one could apply the same logic to Brad's actions surrounding Nancy's disappearance, which was undoubtedly a very stressful time for him.

On the initial day of Nancy's disappearance, Brad told the police about the marital problems he and Nancy were experiencing. Though Brad mentioned that things were somewhat normal for them, he told the police about his affair and the couple's separate sleeping arrangements. As with many of Brad's statements, they required context. Normal to Brad and Nancy while they were in the process of separating was quite different from normal for a happily married couple.

It is hard to imagine the mess Brad would have been in with the police if he had not told them about his affair with Heather Metour. Many spouses avoid discussing an infidelity at all costs. And there have been many spouses and lovers who have been the focus of murder investigations because they lied about an affair. They lied because they did not want to divulge the affair, not because they were involved in the murder. Luckily for Brad, he did not take this avenue. Regardless, the police felt everything he said was a lie, even though he could not have possibly been lying about everything.

Even though Brad reluctantly admitted to an affair, the prosecution felt it was a point that needed to be made. It was not in contention, yet the prosecution asked almost every witness about Brad's affair. The affair occurred years before Nancy death, and it had also been over for years.[cvi] There was no apparent connection to Nancy's death, not even indirectly. Why did the judge allow so much time to be wasted by allowing this line of questioning? How did it meet the relevance criteria for admissibility?

The prosecution refused (and the court concurred) to turn over to the defense any information pertaining to affairs Nancy may have had, even if they were ongoing at the time of her death. The prosecution clearly believed Brad's infidelity from years prior may have been a factor in Nancy's death, yet they failed to see any possible connection or relevance to the victim's possible sexual promiscuity. Regardless, the prosecution pushed the fact that Brad's having an affair was somehow relevant to the murder trial. The connection was never made. Further, the prosecution repeatedly presented undisputed information with no discernable evidentiary value. If the prosecution truly wanted to raise the issue of an affair, why did they not just call Heather Metour to testify rather than ask countless witnesses whether or not they knew of the affair? It was merely an attempt to weaken the character of the defendant. The prosecution could have just as likely asked each witness if they had ever seen Brad kick a dog.

One of the first areas where the police identified discrepancies in Brad's statements pertained to his claims of cleaning the house on the morning of July 12. Brad told police he cleaned the kitchen, bathrooms, and the floors. However, the house looked a mess. Clothes were strewn about. There were boxes throughout the house. Lead Detective for the Nancy Cooper murder investigation, Gregory Daniels, described it as if they were, "…sloppily moving out of the house."[cvii] Add to this speculation, numerous witnesses were telling the police that Brad *never* cleaned while Nancy *always* did the housework.

The Cary Police Department received a lot of their initial information for the case from Nancy's friends. The sources were seen by the police as impartial, though it was certainly a debatable assumption. Many of the statements Nancy's friends provided focused on normal activities of the Coopers. Some of the information contained apparent absolute conclusions about various behaviors utilizing such words as "never" and "always." The police failed to realize how these words are used in everyday speech and how they can be easily misleading, even though not necessarily on purpose. Both words are much weaker than they appear. *Never* does not mean never. *Never* in everyday use means infrequently or less than expected. Here are a few examples of common uses of never to illustrate the point. "My son never takes a shower." Does this mean the woman's son has never set foot in a shower? He does not take a shower 365 days a year? Of course not; it means he rarely takes a shower. He may even take a shower several times a week, but if the child plays in the dirt and runs around, anything less frequent than a daily shower probably seems like never to his mother.

"My husband never takes me out to dinner." Has her husband avoided taking his wife to a restaurant the entire time they have been married? Unlikely. It was not what the wife intended, though there may have been some implied exaggeration in her statement. He likely *rarely* took her out to dinner. *Never* does not always mean never.

"Always" is a very similar word to "never," except it is on the other end of the spectrum. *Always* does not usually mean every time. It means a lot or frequently. "My wife always cuts the grass." Does she cut the grass most of the time? Yes, but she likely does not cut the grass every time. The husband has probably cut the grass at some point during the time they lived in their house. "I always wear sunglasses when I drive to protect my eyes." Has she ever driven a car without sunglasses? Of course she has. However, she goes to great lengths to ensure she wears sun glasses when she drives.

There was no doubt that Nancy told friends and family that she *always* cleaned the house, and Brad *never* helped out. Nancy's friends may have believed this as well. And Nancy may have been correct in her assessment that Brad *rarely* cleaned the house and she *usually* cleaned the house. However, her statement was not literally correct. It was not clear whether the numerous witnesses who told the police what Nancy told them believed her words were literally correct, but they certainly tried to imply it was. Regardless, the police thought the statements were literal. Not one time in Brad and Nancy's life together did Brad ever touch a rag, sponge, or vacuum? This was simply not true. It was a rare occurrence, and it was probably much less frequent than Nancy would have liked, but it was not *never*.

If Brad rarely cleaned, and he claimed he cleaned on July 12, it was not nearly as compelling an argument if he had not once cleaned the house. In addition, with the overt hint of divorce in the air, Brad had made a very recent and very huge improvement in his efforts to help out Nancy. Therefore, it was much more likely Brad would have cleaned something in 2008 than in any other year they were married. It was also more likely he would have picked up the girls from school during the last few months of Nancy's life.

Nancy seemed to resent Brad's attempts at reconciliation, but changes were evident in 2008. The police, and later the prosecution, wanted to pretend this fact was not present because it significantly weakened their already loose link between Brad's activities and Nancy's murder. Brad cleaned prior to July 12, 2008.

The next question at hand, though not directly addressed by the State, focused on Brad's skill level when it came to cleaning. Was Brad good at cleaning? With the exception of Brad, there was probably no one who knew him who would have said he was good at cleaning. For one thing, he appeared to be somewhat of a slob. With Nancy gone, Brad tended to leave dirty dishes in the sink and clothes lying around the house. Brad's top priority was not cleanliness. In order to try to please Nancy, Brad made attempts at cleaning the house.

When Nancy and the girls went on vacation in late June of 2008, Brad bragged to Nancy that he had cleaned the house.[cviii] Upon Nancy's return, she was livid with Brad for the condition of the house. She thought it was a disaster area. And based on pictures taken by the police less than a week later, Nancy's assessment of the condition of the house was more accurate. Brad may have cleaned parts of the house, but overall the house was a mess. Brad's attempts at cleaning left a lot to be desired. Brad was horrible at cleaning.

Once the case turned into a homicide, the Cary Police Department executed a search warrant on the Cooper residence and cars. Upon thoroughly searching the entire Cooper residence and cars, the police found no evidence that

Nancy was murdered in the house. Now there was a complete one hundred and eighty degree turn by the police in their thinking. Brad did clean because they found no evidence. Brad never cleaned, but he cleaned on the day of Nancy's disappearance. Not only did Brad clean, he did an excellent job cleaning the house. The house was a complete mess, but Brad was meticulous in his cleaning around where he *murdered* Nancy.

The guy who *never* cleaned, all of a sudden became the cleaning guru of late night television who can get coffee stains out of a white sweater with steel wool. Or maybe it was blood out of dresses and flooring? Brad's cleaning skills had suddenly taken a big step upward. It was another huge stretch with no evidence to support the theory. The police and prosecution came to the conclusion, not from the facts but from their belief as to who did it. Brad killed Nancy in the house, but there was no evidence of it; therefore, Brad cleaned after the murder. Again, the absence of evidence was their evidence.

The Cary Police Department claimed that it viewed the totality of the circumstances when it determined Brad was a person of interest, but Brad's cleaning claim may have been one of the first chinks in his armor as far as the police were concerned. The police believed he lied about cleaning the house. However, their opinion changed after no evidence was found in the house. Yet they seemed to conveniently forget that Brad had been truthful. It was one of many times their instincts were completely wrong.

Though a competition could probably be held where people voted on which portion of the State's case wasted the most time, Nancy's necklace would have ranked fairly high on most people's list. When Nancy's body was found, she was not wearing a necklace. Jessica Adam signed a statement in October of 2008 indicating that at absolutely no time was Nancy without her necklace. She went on to say at the 2011 trial that the, "…entire time she knew Nancy she wore diamond-studded earrings and a necklace…"[cix]

Apparently the fact that Nancy always wore her necklace somehow implicated Brad in her murder. No matter who killed Nancy, it did not change the fact that she was found without it. The autopsy report concluded Nancy was strangled to death. If she was strangled while wearing her necklace, there would have likely been marks on her neck from the necklace. But there were no marks. The necklace would have been kinked, torn, or damaged in some way, yet there were no indications the necklace was damaged in any way. Nancy was not wearing the necklace when she was killed.

Several other witnesses during the trial testified that Nancy *always* wore her diamond pendant necklace. First off, *always* does not mean always. It means a lot or most of the time. Nonetheless, several of the witnesses for the State claimed she wore a necklace 24/7. Unfortunately, they were not in a position to attest to the fact, since they were not with her all the time. It did not stop them from stating it though. Second, Brad bought the necklace for her in the fall of 2007. She had only had the necklace for approximately nine months. It was a relatively new necklace.

As an aside, why did Nancy *always* wear a necklace purchased for her by someone she despised? Nancy certainly provided Brad with various indicators that she still cared for him. Most women would not continually wear a gift from someone they hated. Was this another example of Nancy sending mixed messages to Brad? Back to *always*.

To disprove *always* in the literal sense as Jessica, Hannah, and others had claimed, the defense only had to find one instance where Nancy was not wearing her necklace. If there was one picture of Nancy without the necklace post fall of 2007, it completely refuted the prosecution's entirely irrelevant line of questioning. What exactly was the necklace supposed to mean to the jury or a reasonable person? Brad killed Nancy, of course. If Nancy wore the necklace one hundred percent of the time, then she had to be wearing it when she was killed. The necklace was found in the house. As a result, Brad must have taken the necklace off of Nancy after he killed her and placed it in a drawer. How many leaps did the jury have to make to equate Nancy wearing a necklace with Brad's guilt? It had no relevance.

During the afternoon before her disappearance, Nancy spent time at the pool with her girls and one of her friends, Hannah Prichard. Since Hannah had never seen Nancy without her necklace, she must have been wearing her necklace while at the pool. Jessica saw Nancy later that evening, and Jessica had also stated Nancy always wore her necklace. Therefore, Nancy had to be wearing her necklace when she got home to meet Jessica. In between Nancy's time at the pool and her arriving home, she stopped at a local grocery store to pick up a few items. Through a little luck and sheer determination, the defense team found a video of Nancy going through the checkout line at the grocery store on the afternoon of July 11. The picture showed Nancy without her necklace. No amount of pictures showing Nancy wearing the necklace negated the significance of one picture of her without it. It only takes finding one black swan to refute the claim there are no black swans. Unfortunately, the prosecution's theory only took one example to prove it incorrect. Any picture of Nancy not wearing her diamond pendant necklace during the last nine months of her life completely refuted their argument, much less one from the day before she went missing. Why would the prosecutors go to such great lengths to push a theory so easily invalidated? The theory did not even provide loose, circumstantial evidence incriminating Brad.

Though the singular picture of Nancy without her necklace negated a portion of the prosecution's theory, it significantly discredited the two key witnesses. Not only did the defense find a picture of Nancy sans necklace, it was in between the time Hannah and Jessica saw her. Unless Nancy took off her necklace after leaving the pool, only to put it back on after a trip to the grocery store, both Jessica and Hannah were wrong about Nancy's having worn the necklace on the Friday before she was killed.

Jessica and Hannah may have merely been mistaken. However, they chose to confidently testify, under oath, that Nancy *always* wore her necklace when they should have only testified to what they had seen. To their own peril, both of them stated emphatically that Nancy always wore her necklace. As a result, Jessica and Hannah lost credibility.

All of the time devoted to proving Nancy *always* wore the necklace was a waste. It was a dead end, and the prosecution should have known it before the trial even started. The prosecutors knew if the defense looked hard enough, they would find evidence of Nancy without the necklace. The prosecutors had to know Nancy did not literally always wear the necklace. They were throwing mud at a wall and seeing what would stick, not exactly the most sophisticated approach, though certainly time-consuming.

The State tried to present Brad as an evil man. Since Brad did not do his fair share of cleaning around the house, it implicated him in murder. He supposedly deprived his wife of money and possessions, yet everything they owned and did pointed to the contrary. The garage and house were filled with stuff. All things purchased by Nancy and Brad. Even so, what would it mean if everything the State presented regarding Brad's character were true? It would mean Brad was not a great husband, but not a murderer. The defense spent countless hours discrediting the information presented.

Unfortunately, the trial was not focused on the law. It was driven by sensationalism and circumstance. The prosecution concealed a marketing campaign under the veil of evidence. Presenting Brad as an adulterer did nothing more than lower the jury's opinion of Brad. Brad's infidelity had nothing to do with Nancy's death. Had his affair happened contemporaneously to her death or the circumstances seemed to be intertwined, then it would have been an appropriate discussion. Nancy had affairs. However, these affairs were dismissed by the prosecution even though one or more of Nancy's affairs may have been ongoing when she was killed.

The prosecution paraded out several witnesses whose testimony was supposed to present context for the Cooper marriage, Brad's behaviors, and details about Nancy. In actuality, the testimony provided biased opinion, was primarily based on hearsay, and on many occasions, it was proven wrong. It was not clear whether many of the witnesses intentionally lied or they so badly wanted what they said to be true, they believed it to be so. Their testimony bogged down the trial and contained very little useful information with almost no evidentiary value.

Though it was one of the longest trials in Wake County history, the prosecution had only one actual piece of evidence: a temporary Internet file. Brad's work computer contained data indicating someone conducted a Google search on the location where Nancy's body was found. The search supposedly took place the day before she went missing. It was only circumstantial evidence, but it was quite compelling. After months of tangents and diversions, it was arguably the only factor that truly mattered in the prosecution's case.

The FBI found the evidence on Brad's computers. During discovery, the court ruled that the defense was not allowed to review the FBI's procedures and protocols for evaluating computers because of national security. The defense was also unable to view the testing the FBI conducted. The court's ruling was basically a blanket denial of the defense's request to review anything the FBI had done on this case.

As part of the defense's case, they called a computer expert, Jay Ward, to testify regarding computer security, evidence Brad's computer had been tampered with, and also to refute many of the FBI's assertions. The State objected to Jay Ward's being called as a computer forensic expert, though they gave minimal notice for their objection. During the debate, Mr. Ward admitted that he was not a computer forensic expert. The State used Mr. Ward's own admission as further grounds for their claim he was not a forensic expert. The court agreed, and Jay Ward was not allowed to testify as an expert on various technological aspects of the case.[cx]

There is a difference between being considered an expert in the business world and in the courtroom. Mr. Ward attested to his opinion of his expertise in the business world rather than in a legal sense. Additionally, there was no basis to claim that he had to even be a forensic expert. Regardless, Mr. Ward's testimony was significantly limited.

The defense had not been able to review the FBI's work. Now, the expert the defense was planning to utilize to refute the FBI's claims was no longer considered an expert. The court had completely limited the defense's ability to counter anything the State had asserted. Fairness had been thrown out the window. Brad's attorney, Howard Kurtz, was beyond appalled. Though it would get worse for the defense, the court's blocking their computer expert was the final straw. Mr. Kurtz referred to Judge Gessner's rulings as, "consistently outside the bounds of prudent jurisprudence."[cxi] He asked for a mistrial, and he also asked the judge to recuse himself. The court denied both requests.

Once Mr. Kurtz's shock wore off, he preceded to find another witness who was a computer forensic expert to fill in the gaps left by the inability of Mr. Ward to fully testify.

Mr. Kurtz submitted a computer forensic expert by the name of Giovanni Masucci. The State moved to prevent Mr. Masucci as a witness, since they were not notified prior to the start of the trial. It was a violation of the discovery rules. The court agreed.[cxii] The defense was not allowed to call an expert to refute the sole piece of evidence indirectly linking Brad to Nancy's murder. The wheels had officially fallen off.

The defense presented several eyewitnesses who had seen Nancy on the morning of her disappearance. They presented alternative theories and even called witnesses to attest to Nancy's infidelities. The testimony may have helped, but it hardly diverted the attention away from the computer forensic evidence. The State presented fairly compelling evidence linking Brad to the murder and all the defense could do was watch. The court had relegated the defense to the role of bystander during the most important part of the trial. It did not bode well for Brad's freedom.

On May 5, 2011, the jury of two men and 10 women found Bradley Graham Cooper guilty of first degree murder.[cxiii] Though most of the jurors have remained silent regarding the case, the foreman stated to various media outlets that the testimony by the FBI agents pertaining to the Internet searches was the primary factor determining their decision.[cxiv] For some, the trial provided closure, but for others it fostered anger and resentment at the legal system.

Chapter 6 – The Evidence…That Matters

The 2011 trial provided more questions than answers. It was more reality television show than reality. Apparently we live in a country where the legal system is based on insinuation and circumstance. The justice for the murder of Nancy Cooper was predicated on her friends' directing the police toward a suspect, ignoring evidence to the contrary, and a prosecutor's office and judge who appeared comfortable with a defendant not able to present a reasonable defense. It was reminiscent of the end scene from the movie *Gladiator* from 2000 where the hero, played by Russell Crowe, fights the evil emperor, played by Joaquin Phoenix, in a death match in the Coliseum. To anyone watching the fight, it looked like a fair competition, but that was far from the case. Prior to the duel, while the hero was still shackled, the emperor stabbed him in the back resulting in a mortal wound. The hero was then placed into his armor, which hid the wound. Though the State fell a little shy of an evil emperor, and Brad did not qualify as a hero, in both situations one side did everything they could to ensure victory, not fairness. From the vantage point of the crowd (jury), it appeared to be a level playing field. Unfortunately, there was no fairness in either situation.

Significant information was missed and ignored by the police and prosecution. It was an embarrassing display of justice. Unfortunately, repeat offenders manipulate the justice system to their advantage. Our justice system often appears to shield the guilty, but it is designed to protect the innocent. And all defendants are supposed to be considered innocent until they are proven guilty. Brad did not receive a fair trial, and though Brad has certainly suffered, so has Nancy's family, as they did not truly receive justice.

The trial only served to muddy the waters. What really happened to Nancy on the morning of July 12, 2008? What did the evidence mean? And who killed a beautiful mother, wife, daughter, and sister for no apparent reason?

Upon analyzing and reviewing almost any homicide, one should start with the people closest to the victim and work his way outward. Spouses, girlfriends, and/or boyfriends are usually first on the list. Love and hate run close together. The passion and emotions within a relationship occasionally turn violent. Very few spouses ever kill their spouse; however, for married people who are murdered, the percentage killed by their spouse is high. On the other end of the spectrum, very few homicides are committed by strangers. Though people do get killed by strangers, it is the least likely scenario. In between the two ends of the spectrum are other family members, lovers, close friends, neighbors, and acquaintances.

In order to attempt to get to the truth of what happened to Nancy, we need to objectively review all of the data points and circumstances surrounding her life and death. The information most relevant to determining who, when, where, why, and how Nancy was killed are the following items: 1) the forensic evidence, 2) the computer evidence, 3) the eyewitnesses, 4) and the statements and actions of the key participants in this case.

When evaluating the forensic evidence, the starting point is the autopsy. Dr. John Butts performed Nancy's autopsy on the evening of July 15, 2008. The body was decomposed with significant infestation. Dr. Butts determined the cause of death as asphyxia by strangulation. The determining factor was most notably the fracture of the right, back part of the hyoid bone in the neck. There was also dark discoloration of the anterior strap muscles and a faint line across the central part of the neck, just over an inch in length. However, there was no mark from a cord or rope, which seemed to indicate that Nancy was manually strangled.[cxv]

Though the poor condition of Nancy's body may have masked injuries, there were minimal indications of a violent death. There were no signs of a struggle or fight. One study of women who were strangled but did not die found that 62% of the victims had no visible injuries.[cxvi] The same study found only 16% of the victims had significant injuries and only 3% required medical attention. Though victims of strangulation who died as a result of their attack have more visible injuries, there are numerous strangulation deaths with no immediately identifiable injuries. In only about one third of homicides by strangulation is the hyoid bone fractured.[cxvii] When the hyoid bone is fractured it has usually been found to be a result of manual strangulation, versus a ligature or rope.[cxviii]

One of the reasons some victims of strangulation do not have visible injuries is because loss of consciousness can occur very rapidly. With consistent, firm pressure on the carotid arteries of the neck, a victim can lose consciousness in approximately six to 10 seconds. Further, it only requires approximately 11 pounds of pressure on the carotid arties to cause a person to pass out.[cxix] For a perpetrator to close off the trachea, thus eliminating the victim's breathing source, it requires around 33 pounds of pressure.[cxx]

There is a significant time differential between how long it takes for a victim to lose consciousness compared to how long it takes to die as a result of strangulation. Consciousness is lost in seconds, but death does not result for three to five minutes.[cxxi] It begs the question, what happens between the time the victim loses consciousness and the time the victim dies? No matter how persistent the killer, it seems unlikely one continues to strangle his victim for almost five minutes after her body has gone lifeless from a loss of consciousness. Maybe in an exceptionally emotional case, a person may continue to strangle the victim for minutes after the person is unresponsive. However, though no less brutal, in most cases the victim's resistance and struggle results in a loss of consciousness occurring much more closely to the time of death than would be expected from a stationary victim with constant, firm pressure on the neck. Otherwise, it is unlikely many perpetrators would continue to strangle someone for several minutes when the victim is lifeless and no longer struggling. To those unaware of the length of time necessary to kill someone via strangulation, it would be simply overkill.

Regardless, someone likely had his or her hands wrapped around Nancy's throat for several minutes. Yet there was also minimal evidence she was strangled. There were no cuts or scratches on her neck. No bruises. On visual inspection, Dr. Butts noted only a fine line across her neck. Nancy was young and healthy. She was in great physical shape, but she put up almost no struggle.

Blood was found under Nancy's fingernails, but the North Carolina State Bureau of Investigation was unable to obtain a DNA sample.[cxxii] However, many times the scratches and bruises on the victim's neck are not a result of the attacker, but of the victim's attempting to loosen the hold on her neck. The subsequent skin or DNA underneath the victim's nails would mostly be her own, though it was probable that some of the DNA found under Nancy's nails was from her attacker. Hopefully, the evidence has been properly secured, which would enable future analysis of the DNA as science continues to advance.

There were many possibilities for why there was no indication of resistance. Nancy could have fought back viciously, but it did not result in identifiable markings on her. The infestation of her body may have masked injuries. She may have been held down or overpowered so quickly that she was unable to resist. She could have been strangled as part of sexual asphyxiation with a partner, as she was found nude with limited explanation for her location and condition.

A toxicological test was conducted as part of the autopsy. The test returned negative results for the presence of cocaine, opiates, or oxymorphone. Caffeine and ethanol (alcohol) were detected. The alcohol level was 60 mg/dL, which equated to a blood alcohol concentration (BAC) of 0.06%.[cxxiii] The autopsy report noted that the presence of alcohol could have been the result of the decomposition process. Notwithstanding this possibility, the alcohol in Nancy's body also could have resulted from her ingestion of alcohol during the last hours of her life.

According to numerous people who were present at the Duncan party on the night prior to Nancy's disappearance, Nancy drank alcohol throughout the evening. People saw her drinking wine and beer. When Jessica Adam asked Nancy to come over, Nancy allegedly replied she was staying put because she had too much to drink.[cxxiv] According to Diana Duncan, Nancy drank four glasses of wine before switching to beer.[cxxv] She did not elaborate on how many servings of beer Nancy consumed.

Nancy arrived at the Duncan party around 6:00 p.m. and left shortly after midnight. During the time she was at the party (6+ hours) she consumed at least five alcoholic beverages, but likely more. Based on Nancy's body weight, alcoholic consumption, and duration of time, her BAC upon leaving the party was probably between 0.15% and 0.25%+ (various inputs, such as type of alcohol consumed, amount of alcohol consumed, and time frame for the consumption result in a fairly wide ranging BAC). By almost any measure, Nancy was intoxicated when she left the party. Nevertheless, Nancy regularly drank alcohol. Much of Nancy's extra-curricular activities involved drinking. As a result, Nancy had a high tolerance for alcohol, which masked the effect the alcohol had on her during the evening.

When Nancy left the party, she had a considerable amount of alcohol in her body. If she were killed shortly after she left the party, she would have had much more alcohol in her system than the toxicology report of 60 mg/dL (0.06%). Once death occurs, the body stops metabolizing alcohol. Therefore, if the time of death was in the early morning hours of July 12, then one would have expected a significantly higher BAC. If one extends the metabolism of the alcohol in Nancy's system until around 7:00 a.m. or 8:00 a.m., her BAC would have been around 0.05% to 0.10%+. This range was consistent with what was found during the autopsy. Thus, if the decomposition process did not generate the alcohol in Nancy's body, the alcohol level found was more consistent with a death shortly after she supposedly went for a run than earlier in the morning.

The toxicology report identified the presence of caffeine. During the trial, the prosecution attempted to draw significance to the caffeine as if it implicated Brad. As with many of their lines of thought, it was never clear how the presence of caffeine meant Brad killed Nancy shortly after the party. Even though Diana Duncan testified that there was no coffee or soda (drinks containing caffeine) at the party, the prosecution believed that caffeine from earlier in the day could have still been in her system shortly after midnight, but not six or seven hours later. However, Dr. Butts stated the caffeine could have been there from days prior to her death, which almost eliminated the value of the presence of caffeine as a barometer for determining the time of death. Further, Nancy could have consumed coffee prior to her run, but there was no indication she did.

According to the autopsy report, Nancy's stomach was empty, except for what may have been part of a red onion. Generally, it takes four to six hours for food to clear the stomach.[cxxvi] As a result, Nancy most likely died more than four to six hours after the last time she ate, which could have been anytime during the party (6:00 p.m. to 12:30 a.m.), but several attendees stated she ate and drank throughout the evening. The absence of food in Nancy's stomach posed another significant obstacle for the theory that Brad killed

Nancy right after she got home from the party. However it was only an obstacle if one based conclusions on the evidence in the case.

The prosecution contended that Nancy vomited up all of the contents of her stomach. Unfortunately, there was absolutely no evidence Nancy vomited near the time of her death. Once again, the prosecutors utilized the absence of evidence as proof it happened. No vomit was found because Brad cleaned everything, destroying any pertinent evidence. Therefore, since no evidence was found, it validated the theory that Nancy vomited upon death. More likely, the absence of evidence of Nancy vomiting would mean she did not vomit. Based on the autopsy, Nancy likely died at least four to six hours after she ate, which was also more consistent with a time of death closer to when she reportedly went for a run.

There was no damage to the vagina, other than from insects post-death. Dr. Butts did not find any indication of a sexual assault. However, he indicated the amount of decomposition of the body could have masked a sexual assault.[cxxvii] There was no information pointing toward any kind of sexual misconduct against Nancy, but it could not be ruled out either.

According to Dr. Butts, Nancy had been dead for days. Upon death, the human body stiffens in about six to 12 hours and then over the course of 24 to 48 hours after death, the muscles begin to loosen.[cxxviii] Dr. Butts stated that there was no stiffening or rigor present when he performed the autopsy. He concluded that the "…decomposed remains… [are] consistent with the time interval she was reportedly missing."[cxxix] He could not provide a more definitive time of death.

Though Dr. Butts' conclusion regarding time of death was vague, two elements from the autopsy report pointed toward a later time of death than what the prosecution contended. Both Nancy's BAC and the absence of food in her stomach pointed toward a time of death more consistent with when Brad stated she went for a run rather than right after she left the party.

Nancy's body was found in a drainage ditch off of Fielding Drive on the outskirts of Cary, North Carolina. The killer or conspirator was present at this location within days of when the police arrived. The killer's car was likely driven to this location leaving evidence behind. The killer also had to get out of the car to throw Nancy's body into the ditch, which would leave additional evidence at the crime scene. Everything around Nancy's body could have potentially identified the killer. Clues were everywhere. Unfortunately, the recent rain adversely impacted the evidentiary value of anything left behind by the killer. Tire tracks and foot prints were present, but due to standing water, treads from the tires and shoes could not be identified.[cxxx]

The muddy conditions of the crime scene significantly impaired the police's ability to capture many aspects of the scene in great detail. As a result, the police were criticized for their handling of the crime scene. It appeared they did not preserve and record all aspects of the scene in a thorough fashion. Notwithstanding the police's lack of thoroughness, they collected hundreds of pieces of potential evidence, to include trash because of its close proximity to the body. They also collected maggots and insects from Nancy's body.[cxxxi] Though the police collected a lot of evidence, they placed a lower priority on much of it, a fact which also heightened the criticism against them.

The crime scene collection process was extensive and comprehensive. The fact that casts were not made of the tire tracks or foot prints at first seemed suspect. However, the condition of the impressions prevented the police from casting them in a useful manner. Further, according to the testimony of Christopher Hill of the City County Bureau of Identification, exact measurements of the foot prints could not be taken because they were distorted by the mud.[cxxxii]

The one reasonably accurate measurement Mr. Hill took was of the distance between the two tire tracks closest to where Nancy's body was found. Because he was unable to cast the tire treads, he could not confirm if the two tire tracks were from the same car. Nevertheless, Mr. Hill indicated that the tire tracks were parallel.[cxxxiii] The two tire tracks were 47 inches apart. Both Brad and Nancy's cars had a similar measurement larger than 47 inches.[cxxxiv] There was no indication the police compared the tire distance measurements against any other cars.

Though the police collected a vast amount of evidence from the crime scene, none of it could be tied to Brad or the Cooper home. The police were unable to link Brad to the crime scene. Since the police did not aggressively pursue any leads other than Brad, it is unlikely the police compared evidence against other potential suspects. As a result, the police did not find anything at the crime scene incriminating Brad or anyone else.

Once Nancy's body was found and likely considered a homicide, the police executed a search warrant on the Cooper residence, 104 Wallsburg Court, in Cary and the Cooper's two cars. The judge signed the search warrant on July 16, 2008.[cxxxv] The search warrant did not specify exactly what the police were trying to find within the Cooper house and cars. The implication within the affidavit for the search warrant was that Nancy may have been killed inside the house and her husband, Brad Cooper, may have been involved.

The search warrant provided the police with the opportunity to thoroughly search what they believed was the scene of the crime. The police combed the home. They removed large bags full of items from the Cooper residence.[cxxxvi] The police seized shoes, bed sheets, and a rug from the foyer.[cxxxvii] Forensic teams scoured the house and cars for anything that could indicate a murder happened in the house. The police took photographs and video of the outside of the house, various rooms, and garage.

During the search, forensic experts utilized reagents, alternate light sources, and other sophisticated techniques for identifying blood, fingerprints, and other evidence indicating a murder occurred in the house.[cxxxviii] The police were also looking for straw, soil or anything that could be linked to the location where Nancy's body was found. Though numerous detectives and forensic experts searched the house for hours and collected dozens of items of potential evidentiary value, the police found no evidence that a murder occurred in the house. The police were unable to find blood anywhere in the house.[cxxxix] The forensic teams were unable to find any blood in either of the Cooper cars, and there was no evidence Nancy's body was ever in the trunk of Brad's car, which was theorized to have been used to transport Nancy's body from the house to Fielding Drive.[cxl]

The police's extensive searches of the Cooper residence and cars netted nothing of any evidentiary value, unless the absence of evidence provided a lead. Based on the results of the police searches, it was unlikely a murder occurred in the Cooper home. And neither of the Cooper vehicles was utilized to transport Nancy's dead body. As a result, Nancy was most likely killed somewhere other than the Cooper home.

Chapter 7 – Chain of Custody

The police executed a search warrant on the Cooper residence shortly after Nancy's body was discovered. As part of the evidence collection process, the police collected several computers, hard-drives, and other technology items. One of the computers seized was Brad's work computer from Cisco Systems, an IBM Thinkpad. Upon review of the work computer, the police found evidence on the computer of a 42 second Google Maps search of the exact area where Nancy's body was found.[cxli] The Internet search was allegedly conducted at 1:14 p.m. on July 11, 2008; the day before Nancy went missing. The computer was attached to the Cisco network in Brad's office at the time of the alleged Google search. Almost the entire case against Brad was based on this one piece of evidence. The rest of the prosecution's case was insinuation and perception.

Due to the compelling nature of the discovered computer evidence, it must be closely scrutinized. The extracted Internet files indicated the search took place on the afternoon of July 11. However, Brad may not have even been in his office at Cisco when the alleged search transpired. A co-worker of Brad's, Greg Migulcci, testified that he and three other co-workers left for lunch with Brad on July 11 between 1:00 p.m. and 1:30 p.m. The five Cisco employees had lunch at Two Guys Grille and returned around 3:00 p.m.[cxlii] Mr. Migulcci was a witness for the State, but he could have also easily been an alibi witness for Brad. The other three employees who joined Brad and Greg Migulcci for lunch could have also provided corroborating evidence for Brad's alibi. The other attendees may have even provided a more specific time for when they left for lunch or other highly pertinent details. It was not clear why the defense did not call the other attendees as alibi witnesses. Further, Brad may have utilized an employee identification card on his way out of the office. He could have been seen by one or more cameras as he departed the Cisco campus. Any one of these items could have potentially discredited the entire viability of the State's primary evidence against Brad. If Brad was not in his office when the alleged search transpired, it would prove conclusively that someone planted evidence of such on his computer.

Though the computer evidence was only circumstantial, it was quite impactful. If the search was conducted by Brad, there was a compelling case against him, even though the other evidence pointed away from him. Without disproving or casting doubt on this evidence, the focus should remain on Brad. If the primary evidence against Brad was flawed, then the killer has not been brought to justice.

The police entered the Cooper residence on the afternoon of July 15, 2008, but Brad's IBM Thinkpad was not powered off until 8:30 p.m. the following day (27 hours later). During July 15 and 16, while the computer was left powered on, it was also hooked up to the Cooper wireless network and Cisco's virtual private network (VPN).[cxliii] The computer was outside the control of Brad Cooper, but the police had not fully taken control of the computer either. Since the computer had not been secured, it was susceptible to contamination. It was a total breach of protocol for securing a computer into evidence.

The Department of Justice Guidelines for digital evidence collection readily identifies the risks of allowing digitally collected evidence to be altered. It specifically addresses the need to disconnect technological devices in order to prevent alteration, which could lead to inaccurate conclusions or result in the evidence becoming unusable.[cxliv] The Cary Police Department's failure to sever Brad's computer from external sources upon collection significantly tainted the integrity of the evidence derived from it.

After 27 hours the police powered down the computer and took it into custody. During the trial, there was limited information provided on the chain of custody of the computer while it was in the custody of the Cary Police Department and the FBI. It was not clear who had possession of the computer at any given time, but there was no information the computer ever left police custody.

The FBI did not make a hash of the IBM Thinkpad until over a month after law enforcement took custody of it. A hash is a method for indexing data.[cxlv] Hashing captures the data at a given point in time. If the data has been altered or reversed, it will not match the hash. Hashes compare two sets of data to ensure integrity (i.e., nothing has changed).[cxlvi] Neither the Cary Police Department nor the FBI had a record of what the laptop looked like forensically upon entering police custody. The computer data could have been changed at any time prior to the hashing, and there would be limited ability to accurately capture or identify those changes.

Though electronic evidence is fairly new to the judicial system, the same evidentiary rules apply. Law enforcement must still ensure evidence is collected and secured properly. The integrity of the IBM Thinkpad was compromised from the beginning. The police failed to properly secure the computer. The overall quality of the evidence was significantly reduced as a result of the police's inability to follow protocol. Nonetheless, just because the police did not follow proper protocols does not mean that tampering occurred, it just means the opportunity existed.

Though the police consistently operated outside of standard protocols regarding the custody of Brad's IBM Thinkpad, the most detrimental aspect was their failure to validate the evidence found. Once the police found the Google temporary Internet files tying the IBM Thinkpad to a search of the location where Nancy's body was found, there were several steps they should have taken to confirm the accuracy of the evidence. It was a murder investigation. No short-cuts should have been taken.

There were two actions the police should have taken without question. The police should have requested the router logs from Cisco to confirm the Google Maps search took place over their routers, since the computer was in the Cisco offices when the search allegedly occurred. Many companies routinely track Internet traffic of their employees. And even companies who do not regularly collect and report on employee Internet usage have the capability to monitor. Cisco is a premier technology company with highly sophisticated internal technology. The company could have easily confirmed or denied the alleged search. If the information provided by Cisco indicated the same search occurred through their routers at the same time as what the police found, there would have been little doubt as to who conducted the search: Brad.

The police should have also requested information from Google on the search in question. The police should have confirmed Google's information matched the information extracted from Brad's computer. Google could have validated or invalidated the alleged search. The police sent other subpoenas and requests to both Cisco and Google during the investigation, but failed to validate the most critical information in the case. Had the police confirmed the search with both Cisco and Google, this case may not have even gone to trial.

If the police had requested computer forensic information from independent third-parties, and the information came back contrary to their analysis, the police would have had a whole new set of issues. First and foremost, it should have alerted them to the fact that Brad was being framed. Someone was attempting to mislead the police by planting evidence. The investigation would have become much more expansive and convoluted. However, since none of the requests were made, it never became an issue.

According to Special Agent Gregory Johnson of the FBI, he was not in a position to request information from Google. He was an examiner on the case, and it was the responsibility of the investigators to seek such information. Agent Johnson stated that he advised Detective Jim Young of the Cary Police Department to request confirmation of the cookie information from Google.[cxlvii] Agent Johnson indicated that Detective Young responded, "I'll take it under advisement."[cxlviii]

What did Detective Young do with this information? Did he chose to ignore the advice and not pass the information along or did he advise Detective Daniels, lead investigator on the Cooper case? The person within the Cary Police Department who made the decision not validate the sole evidence linking Brad Cooper to the murder of Nancy Cooper should certainly be questioned. What was the basis for this decision? What was the downside of requesting this information, as there was tremendous upside to the request? If Detective Young failed to pass this information along, what possible explanation could he have had for not conveying this information to Detective Daniels in a timely manner?

In most instances of this nature, the officer simply made a mistake. He/she was overworked. It slipped through the cracks, or it was an oversight. It would have still been a huge problem, but somewhat understandable. Regardless, it was a failure of the overall department, since it did not have procedures in place to ensure redundancy and oversight of critical tasks. Though the Cary Police Department had accumulated a massive amount of information in the Cooper investigation, they had to be fully aware of the tenuous nature of most of the collected information. It amounted to little evidentiary value. The Google search enabled the police to seek an indictment against Brad. This evidence was critical to prosecuting an alleged murderer.

Detective Young testified extensively during the trial. Though he played dumb with the defense attorney on cross-examination until a related discussion took place between the attorneys and judge, he is an intelligent and knowledgeable law enforcement officer. Even still, he engaged in many questionable actions throughout the Cooper investigation, from destroying Nancy's Blackberry phone and SIM card to his failure to promptly notify Detective Daniels of said destruction. Now, Detective Young was the conduit between the FBI and the Cary Police Department regarding follow-up on the most critical evidence in the murder investigation. If Detective Young failed to properly notify Detective Daniels of the FBI's recommendation, did he forget, believe it was not important, or did he intentionally withhold the information? The last option would normally be almost unthinkable, but Detective Young seemed always to be in the position to undermine potentially exculpatory information.

With the police's failure to validate the most compelling evidence against Brad, where were the Wake County prosecutors? The prosecutors in this case should have demanded validation of the evidence. They were about to put a man on trial and seek life imprisonment. How could they not pursue this lead and avoid accusations of gross negligence? The prosecutors seemed more concerned with figuring out how to silence potential defense expert witnesses than verifying the most critical evidence in this case.

According to statements from the jury foreman, the Google search was the deciding factor in determining Brad's guilt.[cxlix] The judge prevented the defense from tendering experts who could have refuted the forensic evidence and identified the material errors the police made by not validating the Google search. As a result, if the jury heard this information, the verdict may have been different. The judge's ruling likely protected the Cary Police Department and the prosecutors from further embarrassment regarding their dismal handling of this portion of the case.

To better understand the circumstances surrounding the police discovery of the Google search results on Brad's work computer, a more traditional example will help to illustrate the magnitude of the problems with this evidence. Scenario: A woman was stabbed to death with a knife. The police had a suspect, but they did not have enough evidence (probable cause) to arrest him. Upon searching an area near where the woman was stabbed, the police found a knife lying in the middle of a yard. Rather than secure the knife and collect it into evidence, the police chose to leave it there. They placed police tape around the yard, but they did not assign a police officer to secure the area. They came back to the yard 27 hours later and placed the knife into evidence. Forensic testing of the knife determined that the suspect's and victim's DNA was on the knife.

The police were aware of a security camera from the next door business, which pointed toward the yard where the knife was found. They chose not to request the security footage from the company until 10 months later. Unfortunately, the company only kept security camera footage for nine months; therefore, the film had already been destroyed.

The above scenario was, in essence, what the Cary Police Department did with regard to the computer evidence against Brad. To be clear, finding evidence on Brad's computer of a search of the exact location where Nancy's body was found was quite compelling evidence, yet still circumstantial. It would require a very creative story from the defense to innocently explain the search.

As with the knife in the above scenario, the police also failed to secure Brad's computer. It does not mean the defendant did not leave the knife behind after killing the victim, but it does mean someone else could have tampered with it while it was technically in police custody. The same could be said of Brad's computer. It was very shoddy police work.

The police also failed to verify the evidence. Had the police immediately requested the security tapes from the business next door they would have known if anyone tampered with it after the fact. Similarly, the Cary Police Department should have immediately subpoenaed Cisco to verify the search took place through their servers and from Brad's specific portal. The police should have also subpoenaed Google to confirm the authenticity of the search. The police failed to do both, which severely damaged the integrity of the evidence. If they had validated the evidence through one or both companies, it would have produced extremely convincing evidence that Brad conducted the search. They did a disservice to justice by failing to validate what limited evidence they had.

During the time when the police had control of the IBM Thinkpad, but failed to properly secure it, 692 files were altered.[cl] Many of the changed files were a result of routine system updates. Some files were altered due to updates pushed through by Cisco via its VPN. Other files were changed without a clear explanation of cause. Regardless of the origin or explanation for the changes, the integrity of the laptop had been compromised.[cli]

For 27 hours, the police left Brad's IBM Thinkpad connected to his wireless network. The Cooper residence network was encrypted, but with a security level capable of only keeping out completely unsophisticated attempts. Jay Ward, network security expert for the defense, stated that the Cooper security measures were, "…like trying to keep someone out of your house using a screen door."[clii] As a result of the weak security in place at the Cooper home, Brad's laptop was vulnerable to attack during the time it was supposed to be in police custody. The opportunity existed for someone to penetrate the network and Brad's computer. If someone wanted to access his computer, it was certainly possible.

The computer was not protected, and the police did not follow any reasonable protocols to ensure the integrity of the computer. Coupled with vulnerability to tampering, there were a number of anomalies with Brad's IBM Thinkpad that occurred after the police took possession of it. Files had been modified and deleted. The administrative password was changed. There were failed attempts to log into the computer.[cliii] There were a tremendous number of invalid timestamps surrounding the timeframe of the incriminating search. Cursor files associated with the search did not look right, and critical cookies were missing. Malware was also found on the computer. Both computer experts hired by the defense stated that they believed the computer had been tampered with or hacked.[cliv] They believed files may have been externally dropped onto the computer.

When the computer arrived at the FBI for testing, its integrity had already been compromised. The computer had been materially altered since it left Brad's possession and control. However, the FBI did not look into allegations of tampering because it was not asked to do so by the Cary Police Department.[clv] FBI Special Agent Gregory Johnson stated that he did not know why or how files were modified.[clvi] He found no evidence of tampering, yet he did not look for it either.[clvii] Officer David Chappell of the Durham Police Department also examined the Cooper laptop. Officer Chappell examined the modified files and determined that all of the modifications were a result of operating system updates or security updates.[clviii]

One area of concern with the IBM Thinkpad was the amount of invalid timestamps. A timestamp is the time printed by a computer to a specific file, which identifies the time a file was added, modified, and/or deleted.[clix] An invalid timestamp can have several causes, such as a slow network, synchronization issues within the system, delayed web service, or an external attack. On Brad's computer in question, the computer had approximately 98% valid timestamps over the life of the computer, but only 17% of the files had valid timestamps between July 10 and 12, 2008.[clx] Of the 507 Google Map search files, which incriminated Brad, *all* of them had invalid timestamps.[clxi]

When forensic examiners find numerous invalid timestamps, at the very least, they should investigate further. Invalid timestamps can be indicative of tampering. There are normal circumstances that can create invalid timestamps, such as cutting and pasting files or moving an archived file.[clxii] Regardless, invalid timestamps are cause for concern. Timestamps are recorded to two locations on a computer, the Standard Information Attribute (SIA) and the

Filename Attribute (FNA).[clxiii] In most instances, the timestamps should be identical in both sets. When the two sets do not match, such as what happened with Brad's IBM Thinkpad, it is an additional indication of tampering. Since most tools and programs designed to alter computer data only affect the SIA timestamps, a mismatch of the two directories should be reviewed closely.[clxiv] Though he was prevented from testifying in front of the jury, the defense's computer forensic expert, Giovanni Masucci, testified that the number of invalid timestamps during the period in question led him to conclude, "...someone potentially altered the files."[clxv]

The cursor files associated with the Google Maps search in question were all the same. The *create, modified,* and *last accessed files* were identical, but they should have been different. [clxvi] The cursor files were dynamic as the cursor was used to zoom in; therefore, the files should have reflected this change, but they did not. The cursor files were another element of the incriminating Google Maps search that warranted closer scrutiny.

Cookies are files stored on a computer that hold data from a specific website or client.[clxvii] They are created when a browser loads a specific website. The cookies attach to one's browser as a type of tracking device. Cookies make navigating websites easier and serve as a virtual bookmark.[clxviii] No cookies were found associated with the incriminating Google search conducted on Brad's computer on July 11, 2008. Without a cookie, the search cannot be validated within the confines of the computer. Agent Johnson of the FBI was unable to provide an explanation for why there was no cookie corresponding to the alleged search.[clxix] The totality of the anomalies associated with the incriminating search and Brad's laptop in general warrant extensive additional analysis to determine why they exist and what they mean for the lack of reliability of the evidence collected.

The Google Maps evidence linking Brad to Nancy's murder contradicted the State's theory. The State contended that Brad was angry with Nancy after their argument on the evening of July 11 around 7:00 p.m. Nancy humiliated Brad in front of their friends and neighbors. When Nancy arrived home later in the evening Brad confronted her. An ensuing argument resulted in Brad being overcome with rage and strangling Nancy to death. However, Brad supposedly conducted the Google search earlier in the afternoon while he was at work.

Brad supposedly killed Nancy in a fit of rage, yet he had the forethought to identify a location for dumping her body in the event he was to kill her at some later time. Logically, the search should have taken place after he killed Nancy, not prior. The Google search implied planning, as if Brad had thought about killing and disposing of Nancy's body for some time.

If Brad intended to kill Nancy and dispose of the body, he had many options for identifying a dump location. He could have driven around looking for a good place to dump a body. However, this approach would run the risk of someone associating him or his car with the location where the body would ultimately be found. He would have been wise to borrow a friend's car, ride his bike, or utilize some other more subtle way to search for a good location. All of these were viable options for identifying a dump location. It would have been prudent to wait a considerable amount of time between when he surveilled a given area and when the body was dumped. By viewing the surrounding area ahead of time, Brad would have been well versed with the area. Under this scenario, there was no reason for Brad to go online and review the location. In addition, Brad may not have known his mother's middle name (he was unable to recall his mother's name during his custody deposition), but he knew his employer could easily identify all websites he visited and online searches he conducted at any given time.

It was also possible Brad already knew of the location where he wanted to dump Nancy's body. He and Nancy may have looked at lots in the neighborhood for building a new house. Brad was a runner and biker; he could have already been aware of Fielding Drive. As with the previous scenario, there was no need for Brad to view the site online if he was familiar with it.

There was also the possibility Brad was completely unaware of a location to dispose of his wife's body; therefore, he utilized Google Maps to find the right choice. If Brad utilized Google Maps to search for a secluded location he would have spent a considerable amount of time online (significantly more than 42 seconds) browsing areas in and around Cary. Most likely he would have conducted numerous searches trying to find the right location. Where were these searches conducted? Why were they not found? Brad did not just click his heals together and find Brittabby Court off of Fielding Drive in 42 seconds. Brad would have searched extensively within Google Maps to find one or more location options. There was no evidence of other such searches.

Finally, we have the scenario where Brad found the location on Brittabby Court through means undetectable to the Cary Police Department or the FBI. Maybe he did the online searches at a local library. He went undercover as a maintenance man and studied the venue. Regardless, he had his location identified. Yielding to an abundance of caution, Brad decided to review the dump location one more time online. He used his work computer from the office because he thought that it was less likely to be detected. In what amounted to a total of only 42 seconds online, Brad compromised his entire recognizance mission. What did Brad gain during the online review? Nothing. The picture was outdated. As of June, 2014, the picture for Brittabby Court on Google Maps was taken in October of 2007. In July of 2008, it could have been an even older picture. Because the area was a new development, it was constantly changing. There was minimal benefit to reviewing an old image of the location.

The actual search itself also defied logic. During the 42 seconds he was online, Brad completed the follow tasks: 1) typed "googlemaps.com" into the browser, 2) switched Google Maps from the map view to the satellite view, 3) typed the zip code "27518" into the search box, 4) moved the screen to the east until it hovered over Brittabby Court, 5) clicked the mouse six times to zoom in the view, and finally, 6) viewed the picture for two seconds.[clxx] Using a high-speed Internet connection, I attempted to replicate this search under various scenarios to see if it was possible and to better understand what could be achieved by viewing the consecutive images. Without any regard for where the zoomed-in view finally landed, I was able to complete the above six steps in about 18 seconds. However, if I completed the same steps, but just waited for the web pages to load before moving to the next step, it took me about 29 seconds. Under this second scenario I did not evaluate the individual screens or re-orient the cursor during drill-downs.

By just observing the satellite imagery on each successive zoom-in, completing the above steps took close to 40 seconds. Each of these scenarios assumed the starting point was exactly where it needed to be for me to zoom-in each consecutive time without having to reorient the satellite view to the proper location. This was not the case when the alleged search was conducted as the user had to move the map east. Even if the location where Nancy's body was found was close to the center of zip code 27518 on Google Maps, it would have required reorientation during the zoom-in phase of the above six steps.

With multiple practice attempts and extreme familiarity with the Cary/Fielding Drive area on Google satellite map, I completed the task in 45 seconds. I learned nothing about the location that I did not already know (as the only way I could find the location so quickly using Google Maps was because I was so familiar with its location and proximity to other landmarks and streets around Cary). Based on my repeated attempts, it seems nearly impossible for anyone to complete the above six steps in 42 seconds under the parameters of a legitimate search. The online search provided limited to no detail about the Fielding Drive location and the amount of steps necessary to zoom-in on the location precluded anyone from studying or evaluating it. When actually replicating the search, it was not feasible, and it made no sense.

The FBI claimed there was no evidence of tampering with the computer, yet they also stated that they did not specifically look for evidence of tampering; therefore, how much validity did their assurances have? They did not find what they were not looking for. Between the time of Brad's arrest and the trial, the prosecution had to be aware of the defense's tampering accusation. Why did they not have the FBI forensically review the computer to determine if it had been compromised? The defense presented two computer expert witnesses who stated that they believed the computer had been tampered with or altered in some fashion. Though experts tend to disagree one cannot just dismiss or explain away all of the unusual characteristics surrounding the Google Maps search. Brad's IBM Thinkpad was likely compromised by someone who externally planted files on his computer, and it may well have occurred while it was in the custody of the Cary Police Department.

Have we just moved into the conspiracy realm? For starters, a conspiracy is nothing more than two or more people conspiring to break the law. If the person who planted the evidence was not Nancy's killer than yes, it was a conspiracy. Nonetheless, if the killer planted the files then there was no conspiracy, but a murder followed by someone framing another person for the crime.

If the computer was compromised, who hacked into it? The police had custody of the computer from July 15, 2008 onward. They clearly had the opportunity and means. However, the police have a legal duty to protect evidence.

They are generally considered unbiased within an investigation. The likelihood someone in the Cary Police Department planted evidence on the IBM Thinkpad is highly remote. Though crooked police officers have obtained forced confessions and planted evidence, it is nonetheless a rare occurrence.

With regard to the integrity of Brad's computer, the chain of custody was weak and poorly documented. They did not properly secure the computer and records of who had access at any given point were less than ideal. Though the police did a poor job overall with the investigation, *most* of it appeared to be incompetence and ill-conceived conclusions. Planting evidence on a computer is intentional, illegal, and career-ending for a police officer. Nonetheless, Detective Young destroyed potentially exculpatory evidence when he wiped Nancy's Blackberry phone and SIM card. And there was a legitimate case for the maneuvers to have been intentional. Furthermore, the same police officer was instructed by the FBI to verify the Google Maps search by obtaining the cookie information from Google. He either failed to convey the information to the appropriate persons or a decision was made to not validate the information. Either way, the same officer was again in a pivotal position where the wrong decision was made. Though Detective Young played dumb on cross-examination, exhibiting a very unprofessional side, there was no indication he had sufficient computer expertise to plant the evidence on Brad's computer. There was no information pointing toward any law enforcement personnel as having conducted such evidence tampering. It is a very remote possibility, and the option is only based on opportunity and poor conduct throughout the investigation rather than any evidence pointing toward such a conclusion.

The next possibility for a potential computer hacker was Nancy's friends and neighbors. In a typical investigation this would not be a reasonable consideration. However, the friends and neighbors in this case did not act as one would expect law-abiding citizens to act. Friends were misleading the police, providing half-truths, and completely comfortable with testifying under oath to things they would have no way of knowing. Friends and neighbors believed Brad was guilty because he did not make eye contact, wore a hat, or walked in an unusual manner. All clear signs of guilt...to them. Nancy's best friend, Hannah Prichard, provided the prosecutors with a clarifying statement because she felt her new information was so important to the investigation. In her follow-up statement, she stated that the earrings Nancy always wore were screw back. Screw back earrings are more difficult to remove, which somehow implicated Brad. Unfortunately for the State and Hannah's credibility, the earrings were pressure backed, which she confirmed by viewing them during the trial. She turned out to be completely wrong again.[clxxi] Friends and neighbors were *creating* evidence against Brad.

The Coopers' friends and neighbors supposedly knew what happened to Nancy, and they were not going to sit idly by as the police tried to figure it out. They were willing to go to great lengths to ensure the police focused on Brad. The police indicated that extra-marital affairs were important to the investigation. Friends and neighbors spewed all the information they had on any affair Brad had or may have had. The Cooper's neighbor, Craig Duncan, testified that

Brad told him of a time he slept with his boss's wife. Mr. Duncan was fully aware that the story Brad told him was from before he was married, but he felt it was not misleading to omit that portion of the story.[clxxii] Mr. Duncan regurgitated the story as if Brad openly bragged about cheating on Nancy, when it was not the case. Neither he nor the prosecution was concerned about his testimony being misconstrued. Friends and neighbors were not just being helpful to the investigation; they were doing everything they could to influence it. They provided affidavits and testimony, which were at best disingenuous.

With regard to Nancy, friends and neighbors painted her as a quasi-saint while withholding any negative information they possessed. They refused to divulge information unfavorable to Nancy, even if it were true. Manipulating law enforcement was something they were willing to do. When Brad was not initially arrested, how far were they willing to go to implicate him?

Planting evidence is clearly against the law. The statements and actions of many of Nancy's friends and neighbors pushed the bounds of illegality, though it was in the gray area. Stepping clearly over the line would have been another level. Yet, many friends believed Brad was a killer who may get away with murder. Fabricating evidence that would merely help convict a guilty person could be justified. The opportunity and motive were present. Similar to the possibility of the police hacking Brad's computer, there was no evidence directly pointing toward any of Nancy's neighbors or friends. However, their cumulative actions and statements clearly made them suspect.

The most likely person to have planted evidence on Brad's computer was the killer or his/her accomplice. *This does not rule out the possibility that the killer was a friend or neighbor.* There was a very strong motive to divert the police away from the actual killer and onto Brad. With fairly clear evidence of computer tampering, a compelling motive and opportunity (weak network security), the remaining component was the ability to complete the hacking. With Cary's close proximity to RTP, one of the premier technology areas in the country, the capability was everywhere.

Chapter 8 – What Eyewitnesses?

Eyewitness testimony has traditionally been considered the most convincing evidence presented in a criminal trial. The primary factors involved in assessing an eyewitness testimony are usually proximity, lighting, bias, and the witness's confidence. With close proximity and reasonable lighting, a disinterested eyewitness is almost irrefutable. Under those circumstances, a confident and articulate eyewitness will trump almost all other evidence presented in a criminal case.

With the advent of DNA testing, the pedestal on which eyewitnesses were placed has begun to show significant cracks. DNA testing has demonstrated that eyewitness testimony has resulted in numerous false convictions. In many cases, the eyewitnesses were simply mistaken.

The irony of eyewitness testimony is that juries and judges often place greater emphasis on the testimony if the eyewitness is more confident in his conclusions. However, confidence is not a reliable indicator of accuracy.[clxxiii] Eyewitness confidence can stem from many factors, with the positive reinforcement of the police as one of the strongest drivers of eyewitness confidence. When a police detective agrees with a witness, it significantly increases confidence, while witnesses generally have lower confidence levels when their identification differs with the detective's theory. In one study, witnesses who did not receive affirmation on their identification had average confidence levels below 50% whereas witnesses who received favorable feedback had confidence levels in excess of 70%.[clxxiv]

Over the years, numerous convictions driven primarily by eyewitness testimony have been overturned through the use of DNA testing. In many of those cases the witnesses were extremely confident in their testimony, making statements such as, "There is absolutely no question in my mind."[clxxv] Statements such as this convey a powerful message almost impossible for juries to disregard or even mitigate. And in some cases, the witness was wrong.

There are a variety of reasons why people incorrectly identify persons as perpetrators of crimes against them, including errors in how the brain recalls memories, police procedural errors, crime scene conditions, and stress during the incident. Most people view a person's memory as being similar to a recording device where, once the mind has recorded an event, it can access the memory and recall a precise replica.[clxxvi] In actuality, researchers have found that memories are reconstructed each time they are accessed. The reconstruction can be affected by the situation in which the memories are being recalled, the audience and the manner in which the questioner elicited the response.[clxxvii] As a result, a person's memory can be affected or changed based on how the individual reconstructs the event.

The brain's ability to recall a memory is far from infallible. Studies have demonstrated that not only do people make mistakes in recreating actual memories; people may actually unintentionally create false memories. Witnesses also confuse memories by including information they did not witness, but were stated by law enforcement or others individuals. In one study, the organizers utilized detailed information from participants' family members in order to craft three true stories and one false story from each participant's childhood. About one third of the participants believed the false story to be true and created false memories to help support the untrue story. And even after the participants were told the story was made up, about 25% of those still claimed they remembered the story.[clxxviii]

Over the last 30 years, over 2,000 studies have been conducted regarding various elements of eyewitness testimony, accuracy, and usefulness.[clxxix] Many of these studies depict a bleak picture for eyewitnesses. In one study, active duty military personnel were placed into an intense interrogation for 30 minutes where they were able to clearly see and hear their interrogator. After the interrogation, participants were exposed to extreme conditions, such as partial food and sleep deprivation for two days. At the end of the two days, the participants were tested on their ability to identify their interrogator from a photo line-up. Only 62% of the participants accurately identified either the presence or absence of their interrogator from the photo line-up.[clxxx]

Though one would expect trained military personnel to achieve higher success rates for identification, their lack of sleep and inadequate nutrition factored into the outcomes. Sleep deprivation and extreme hunger can result in blurred vision and an inability to concentrate, thus significantly reducing a person's ability to accurately identify an individual.[clxxxi] Yet it is still surprising the participants did not fare better.

Some of the limitations regarding eyewitnesses stem from how the brain works and how people remember events and persons. How law enforcement elicits the information affects memory and recollection as well. The adverse impact law enforcement has can be improved as various studies and observations guide law enforcement on how they should handle eyewitnesses. There are many aspects of a witness interview and the identification process that may unintentionally influence a witness one way or another. A police detective could provide non-verbal clues to a witness that may validate certain answers while discouraging others. Also, the tone, inflection and other elements of the detective's presentation could easily sway a witness toward a given answer. This aspect of police interviews applies not just to eyewitness identification, but to all aspects of the police's role in eliciting information.

Another aspect where law enforcement may inadvertently affect a witness's conclusions is through a police line-up. Though some police line-ups utilize actual persons, the majority use photographs. Line-ups usually consist of a suspect and four or five fillers.[clxxxii] The line-ups can be simultaneous where the eyewitness looks at all of the pictures or persons together, or it can be conducted sequentially where the eyewitness views one picture or person at a time. Simultaneous line-ups seem to be more accurate as the witness compares one picture to the other utilizing relative judgment. Sequential line-ups utilize absolute judgment where the individual evaluates each picture against his memory of the perpetrator. Unfortunately and shockingly, the Cary Police Department failed to use photo line-up arrangements for some of the eyewitnesses in this investigation.

During the 2011 trial, the prosecution went to great lengths to illustrate the depth of the Cary Police Department's investigation into Nancy Cooper's death. In what seemed like weeks of testimony, investigators provided excruciating detail on Brad's movements while he was in Harris Teeter on the morning of July 12, even though it was not clear what it demonstrated. The police talked to countless *witnesses*, and many of them were interviewed multiple times, though the information they possessed provided minimal value. Nevertheless, there were many instances where the police failed to follow-up on potential leads that did not support the "Brad did it" theory. One of the most detrimental aspects of the investigation was how the police handled the eyewitnesses who claimed to have seen Nancy jogging on the morning of July 12.

In response to the news coverage and missing person fliers, 16 people contacted the Cary Police Department claiming they saw Nancy or someone who looked like Nancy jogging in the Lochmere area of Cary on the morning she went missing.[clxxxiii] The eyewitnesses directly contradicted the police's theory regarding what happened to Nancy. The police's theory cannot be true without all of the witnesses being wrong.

If 16 witnesses called into the police department stating they saw Brad driving on Fielding Drive on the morning of July 12, investigators would have been knocking on their doors within minutes. There would have been photo line-ups. There would have been extensive interviews and sworn affidavits. Instead, many of the witnesses who claimed to have seen Nancy were interviewed over the phone and months after the fact. Other eyewitnesses were interviewed by patrol officers, not detectives.

On the morning of July 12, 2008, Rosemary Zednick, a retired executive assistant from Alltel Communication, was walking her dog down Lochmere Drive. As she stopped to untangle her dog's leash she looked up to see a female run past on the bike path. Ms. Zednick said "Hi," and the runner responded in kind.[clxxxiv]

After seeing a missing person flier for Nancy, Ms. Zednick called the Cary Police Department to report that she may have seen Nancy running the previous morning. She described the jogger as 5'9", tan, 135 to 145 lbs., and dark hair pulled back. She wore a light colored top with a pair of dark colored shorts.[clxxxv] Since the police had not returned her calls, Ms. Zednick continued to call the police several other times over the next few weeks. She also stopped at one of the police checkpoints in her neighborhood (set up to help locate Nancy Cooper when she was still missing) where she spoke to a patrol officer.

On October 14, 2008, the day before she was set to testify in the Cooper custody case, two detectives finally interviewed Ms. Zednick at her house.[clxxxvi] It had been over three months since she contacted the police. During one of her conversations with law enforcement, Ms. Zednick indicated that the jogger may have worn an iPod. It was not clear whether Ms. Zednick referred to the iPod voluntarily or if she had been specifically asked about it. A police officer may have insinuated Nancy was wearing a device to listen to music and she agreed. Regardless, this was what the police needed- something to invalidate Ms. Zednick's claim because the police believed Nancy was not wearing an iPod.

Probably the most credible and reliable witness who claimed to have seen Nancy jogging was Curtis Hodges. On his way to work at a Food Lion grocery store, he saw a woman who looked like Nancy jogging in the Lochmere area. He saw her running on Kildaire Farm Road heading toward Penny Road just before he got to the golf course, which was a couple of miles from the Cooper home. On the following Monday, July 14, Mr. Hodges saw Nancy's picture on a missing person flier. As a result, he called the police. The police did not contact him until mid-October, three months later.[clxxxvii] The police chose to speak to Mr. Hodges on the phone rather than in person. The police never provided him with a photo line-up or even a picture of Nancy to evaluate.[clxxxviii] The police utterly failed to adequately investigate this lead.

During the 2011 trial, Mr. Hodges described the jogger as a woman in her mid-30's, wearing a white top with a pair of dark shorts. He passed within 25 feet of her as he drove by. She was jogging on the sidewalk. He stated under oath that he was 90% confident the woman he saw was Nancy.[clxxxix] Though confidence does not correlate with accuracy, his statement was in spite of the fact his observations directly contradicted the police's theory of events. Undoubtedly, the police tried several times to convince Mr. Hodges he saw someone other than Nancy. Mr. Hodges did not know Nancy, but he had seen her while he was working (at the Food Lion grocery store) several times. Mr. Hodges described himself as not good with names, but good with faces.[cxc]

The Cary Police Department received several other reports from people who claimed to have seen Nancy running. Some of the witnesses spoke to police officers. Others were not called back for weeks or, in some cases, months. There were likely others who contacted the police and never heard back. Why did the police ignore eyewitnesses and treat them differently than the other witnesses in this case?

The entire handling of the eyewitnesses in this case was inept and mind-boggling. Rosemary Zednick was only interviewed by detectives after the defense publicized her. The detectives interviewed her on the eve of her testimony in the custody case regarding the Cooper children. From the trial testimony, it appeared the police, and later the prosecutors, thought she was seeking publicity or attention. It well may have been the case, but it does not mean she was lying or wrong. The police may have thought she did not see Nancy because Ms. Zednick claimed the woman she saw was wearing an iPod, and the police *knew* that Nancy never ran with an iPod. Regardless, neither of these items was justification for not following-up with a key witness. According to her testimony, she spoke to someone from the police department when she reported what she saw and again when she stopped at a checkpoint set up to find Nancy.[cxci] Did the detectives think they had her full story? Was her truthfulness assessed during the phone call and discussion on the street, or was further investigation necessary? The police had not begun to thoroughly evaluate Ms. Zednick until three months after Nancy's murder.

Curtis Hodges was not even interviewed in person. Any training or class taught on interviewing will clearly state that all critical or potentially important interviews should be done in person. When talking on the phone, the interviewer misses out on the non-verbal clues the witness is providing. The witness could be distracted. The interviewer has less control of the interview when it is conducted on the phone. The detectives in this case were fully aware of all of this. They chose to downgrade the eyewitnesses as superfluous to the case. One could argue the detectives were completely incompetent, but that does not appear to be the case. When listening to Detective Daniels' testimony, he appeared more than competent, though he may have made many mistakes in this case. And the handling of the eyewitnesses was likely a huge judgment error. The Cary Police Department detectives believed Brad killed Nancy before she went running. As a result, the eyewitnesses had to be wrong.

If 16 witnesses supposedly saw Brad Cooper on Fielding Drive on the morning of July 12, 2008, there would have been little to no debate over who killed Nancy. The trial would have been shortened by weeks, if it would have even gone to trial. Though eyewitnesses have been proven to be unreliable at times, who would have been fighting for Brad's innocence in the face of so many witnesses? Who could discredit over a dozen eyewitnesses? Yet, it happened in this case. The witnesses were relegated to a sideshow.

The eyewitnesses in this case did not prove Brad was innocent. Their identifications proved that Nancy went jogging on the morning of July 12, and the entire basis for the State's theory was wrong. Brad still could have killed Nancy, but almost every one of his suspicious behaviors and statements would no longer be considered suspicious. The prosecution's entire case was predicated on 16 eyewitnesses being wrong. They were all simply mistaken.

The detectives never evaluated the eyewitnesses in an unbiased manner. Their actions clearly demonstrated what conclusions the police had already made. Many aspects of the investigation were wrong and misguided, but the handling of the eyewitnesses was utterly destructive to the police's credibility. Once it was clear that numerous eyewitnesses were disregarded by the investigators, the entire handling of the case should have been called into question. The eyewitnesses provided impartial, direct evidence, which refuted the police theory in this case. And the police failed to respond in a manner consistent with how they handled other key witnesses. The police did not call Brad on the phone to get his story. The police did not wait for Nancy's friends to stop a police officer on the street to provide information. The detectives sought them out, in person and quickly. The police had tunnel vision. Brad did it. And anything to the contrary was not seen as valuable information.

Chapter 9 – Brad, Part I

Detective Gregory Daniels of the Cary Police Department
arrived at the Cooper residence in the late afternoon of July
12. He was a seasoned detective who displayed competence
and an ability to size up a situation. Articulate and
confident, he was later chosen as the lead investigator for the
murder investigation. Though Detective Daniels may have
walked into the Cooper household with an open mind, Brad
seemed to sway him one way quickly. Upon meeting Brad,
Detective Daniels noticed red rub marks on the back of
Brad's neck. Brad was unusually tired, but Detective
Daniels expected him to be amped up.[cxcii] Not knowing what
had happened and still treating the situation as a missing
person's case, Detective Daniels asked Brad a series of
questions. Likely, during this initial interview, Detective
Daniels had a pretty good feeling Brad was involved in
Nancy's disappearance. It may have been just a hunch or a
gut feeling, but something did not seem right. The house
was a complete mess, but Brad said he had been cleaning all
day. Brad described his marriage as normal, but said he
slept in a separate bedroom from his wife.

Much the way Brad's demeanor and social awkwardness
caused many of his friends and neighbors to think he had
something to do with Nancy's disappearance, Detective
Daniels picked up on the same non-verbal indicators.
However, Detective Daniels was a trained and experienced
investigator. As a result, he could articulate his suspicions.
Brad claimed that he slept in the girls' room, yet his bed
looked like someone had slept in it. Nancy supposedly slept
in the master bedroom, but her bed looked like no one slept

in it the night prior. As any good detective would do, Daniels soaked in every detail of the scene. He noticed anything out of place. As he received information gleaned from friends and acquaintances and compared it to what Brad had told him, additional inconsistences came to light.

Detective Daniels may have had preconceived notions about what happened to Nancy prior to interviewing Brad and assessing the house. Though still open-minded, he may have had a hunch before he even got involved in the case. It may have been a result of his law enforcement experience, and in most instances, it helped him. But what if things he observed incorrectly validated what he had already believed? Detective Daniels did not find a grieving husband. He did not find an immaculate house as one would expect to find in the middle-to upper-class Lochmere area in Cary. He found what one would expect to find entering a home in a crime-ridden neighborhood. Clothes were strewn about. Beds were unmade. The house was a mess.

Police spend a lot of their time dealing with criminals. A large percentage of criminal activity takes place in a small percentage of a given geographic location, and a lot of it is a result of a small contingent of the population. Police officers typically enter a home to investigate a crime or potential crime. When they enter the homes of drug dealers, car thieves, and committers of various felonies, they find a mess. There is disorganization, bugs, and a lack of respect for their living space. When Detective Daniels entered the Cooper residence that was exactly what he found. This is not to suggest clean and middle class people do not commit serious crimes; they do. Nevertheless, police do not spend most of their time investigating a former NFL star who stabbed his ex-wife to death or a businessman who dumped his wife and unborn child in the ocean. They spend a majority of their time fielding calls from the down-trodden.

The Cooper residence fit the expectation of a crime scene or the home of a criminal for many police officers, and it may have for Detective Daniels as well. Add to this, Brad was not known for his social skills. He was awkward and not overly skillful at explaining things to people. His word choice and delivery differed from the average person. These traits often made people feel uncomfortable. When someone makes another feel uncomfortable, he has a tendency not to like the person. Further, Brad was dealing with accusations by Nancy's sister earlier in the afternoon and friends and neighbors in front of his house. It affected Brad's demeanor.

What at first appeared to be a detective engaging the husband of a missing woman quickly turned into a suspicious situation. Though it is hard to assess how much impact what Brad heard affected his behavior and statements, it was present. Detective Daniels was unaware of this. Maybe Brad should have told him what was being said about him, though it could have been quite detrimental depending on how Detective Daniels interpreted the information. Regardless, Brad was immediately on the defensive and his demeanor showed it. Coupled with Brad's lack of social acumen, he must have appeared abnormal. Things were not as they should have been in the Cooper residence, and Detective Daniels keenly absorbed it all.

Brad did not get a second chance to make a first impression. Brad may have already been doomed. Little clues could have had a huge impact on the focus of the investigation. Detective Daniels believed the condition of the beds were not consistent with what Brad had told him. This one item could have potentially driven the entire investigation; however, Detective Daniels wisely stated during the trial that it was the totality of the circumstances guiding the investigators.[cxciii] However, all humans are prone to error, and people are especially good at emphasizing items that validate their beliefs, while conveniently ignoring items in conflict with their notions.

Horoscopes are a perfect example. In one's horoscope there could be five statements that have nothing to do with one's life, but if there is one phrase that connects to the person, he is a believer. The horoscope is accurate. The same problem arises in scholarly research. Researchers over-emphasize findings consistent with their hypothesis and mitigate findings that contradict what they expected. This human limitation can easily be countered by having an independent third-party review the findings. Otherwise, the conclusion will most likely be determined by the persuasiveness of the presenter rather than the merit of the theory or concept. It does not appear the Cary Police Department ever arranged for an independent review of their conclusions in this case.

What if one or more of Detective Daniels' initial conclusions were wrong, such as the condition of the beds? It could have changed the entire direction of the investigation. "The bed [Nancy's bed] looked like it hadn't been slept in," according to Detective Daniels testimony.[cxciv] He made this observation on the afternoon of Nancy's disappearance. Though the detectives on the Cooper case tried to portray the investigation as impartial and open to pursuing all avenues, Detective Daniels' preliminary assessment indicated he thought something kept Nancy from going to bed the previous night. He likely believed Brad had something to do with it.

A made bed does not look like it has been slept in, though Detective Daniels was not referring to a made bed. Nancy's bed was unmade and messy. On the contrary, an unmade bed looks like someone has slept in it. And Nancy slept in her bed at some point. Even if she did not sleep in the bed on Friday night, the night prior to her disappearance, she most likely slept in the bed on Thursday night. If this was the case, Nancy slept in the bed approximately 36 hours before Detective Daniels evaluated it. Would a bed look significantly different if it were slept in 12 hours ago versus 36 hours ago? Would there be a discernable difference? Not likely. The Cary Police Department did not perform some equivalent of Carbon-dating on the time since someone had slept in the bed. It was merely Detective Daniels' observation and lay opinion, an opinion that never should have been allowed in a courtroom as he was not an expert on assessing the impact a sleeping person has on bedding or a bed.

Detective Daniels' observation appeared to be biased or pre-determined. He likely already suspected Brad of involvement in Nancy's disappearance; hence, he focused on items supporting his conclusion. As stated, it is human nature to emphasize and remember supporting information and ignore or mitigate conflicting circumstances. This phenomenon may be natural, but it is very dangerous within an investigation as it leads to investigators ruling out alternative scenarios and new evidence. The Cary Police

Department seemed to lack investigators who were tasked with punching holes in conventional wisdom and taking adversarial positions. Had the Cary Police Department had someone review the case in an unbiased manner, it would have forced investigators to strengthen their theory through the identification of flaws in their reasoning. In the end, the review would have provided great preparation for trial as the investigative team would have been already aware of counter arguments.

The police asked Brad what Nancy wore to the cookout on the night prior to her disappearance. They wanted a clothing item she had recently worn so that one of the K-9 dogs could attempt to track her scent. Brad initially indicated that Nancy wore a blue, knee-length summer dress with thin straps.[cxcv] To confirm the color of the dress Nancy wore, Brad asked Craig and Diana Duncan, who were both at the cookout. Apparently, Brad asked the Duncans if Nancy wore a *black* dress the preceding night, though Diana had earlier in the evening told a police officer the dress was blue. Regardless, somehow through discussions with Brad and the Duncans, the police concluded that the dress was black.[cxcvi] At trial, Diana testified that Brad somehow tricked her into believing the dress was black when she knew it was not, though her explanation as to how and why she changed her description of the dress only confused the matter.[cxcvii]

Another person present at the July 11 cookout was Damia Tabachow. Damia also initially thought Nancy's dress from the evening was black, until her husband Ross told her the dress was teal green.[cxcviii] For some reason, no one other than Ross Tabachow seemed to confidently remember what Nancy wore to the party. There was much confusion.

However, the confusion and varying memories were acceptable to law enforcement, except as it pertained to Brad. Apparently, his confusion was deliberate.

On Sunday, July 13, the day after Nancy went missing, Brad handed Detective Young the *green* dress they had been searching for the prior day.[cxcix] The blue turned black dress had now become green. Brad allegedly advised the police that the dress had been washed because Nancy spilled something on it.[cc] Though others in the Cary Police Department believed Brad stated he washed the dress, according to Detective Young's testimony, Brad indicated the dress had been washed, but he did not specify who washed it.[cci] Brad thought the dress had been washed, which the police construed as incriminating. The detectives believed that Brad led the police away from the actual dress Nancy wore; therefore, he had time to wash it before turning it over to the police.

Under the police theory, Brad spent the morning cleaning and doing laundry in order to remove evidence of a murder, yet he forgot to wash the dress Nancy was wearing when she was killed. As a result, he lied about the dress she wore and then tricked several other attendees into believing his version of what Nancy wore. He then waited for the police to leave and laundered her dress. After washing it, he gave it to the police, confidently believing his washing skills removed any possibility of evidence from the dress. Brad also pretended that he had told the police all along that the dress was green when he had in fact referred to it as blue.

The police did not have her dress nor did they know the precise color of it because other witnesses were also unable to remember the specifics. Yet after supposedly murdering his wife while she was wearing this dress, Brad voluntarily turned it over to the police for forensic analysis. There was no reason for him to produce it, since the police did not even have an accurate description of it.

Brad had also told Detective Young the reason the dress had been washed was because Nancy spilled something on it. The police questioned several witnesses as to whether or not they noticed a stain on Nancy's dress during the cookout. No one remembered Nancy spilling anything on her dress. Several party attendees added that Nancy would have definitely made a big deal out of a stain, and she had not done so. Brad was supposedly lying about the stain as well. There was no stain. Brad must have used the stain as a cover story for why he washed the dress.

It appears Brad was mistaken. The dress was not laundered. Detective Young noted deodorant stains on the dress.[ccii] When the Cary Police Department had the dress forensically tested they found a "small grease-like stain."[cciii] Brad may have been wrong about the dress having been laundered, but he was correct regarding the stain. Brad had not washed the dress to conceal evidence.

There was much confusion surrounding the dress Nancy wore on the night before she disappeared. No one seemed to remember what she wore. The actual color of the dress is teal. Teal is described as a shade of bluish-green. Brad's recollection of the color of the dress appeared to be accurate in hindsight. He originally referred to it as blue, but once he found the dress he referred to it as green. In what seemed like a contradiction was in fact an accurate description of a blue-green dress. This did not stop the prosecution from trying to confuse the jury into thinking Brad deceived the police by changing his description of the dress.

Though Brad thought the dress had been laundered, it had not. If Nancy had been killed while she wore the dress, there was no evidence to validate the theory. Unfortunately, for the police and prosecution, the forensic testing of the dress found no blood or bodily fluids on it.[cciv]

On July 15, a female body was discovered not far from the Cooper residence. Once the medical examiner determined it was Nancy, Detective Daniels informed Brad. He then asked Brad if he could search the residence. Brad asked if he was a suspect. Detective Daniels indicated that "bells went off when Brad asked if he was a suspect."[ccv] The police repeatedly questioned Brad, asking many of the same questions. They had identified no other suspects or explanations for what could have happened to Nancy. The Cary Chief of Police was on television stating it was an *isolated incident* and people should feel safe. Now, they were asking to search the Cooper house again. Yet, Detective Daniels was surprised Brad thought he was a suspect? Once again, Brad's statements and actions did not match up with what the police expected. Further, friends, neighbors, and even Nancy's sister had accused him of hurting Nancy. Of course Brad thought he was a suspect.

Chapter 10 - Brad, Part II

"As you sit here today, do you stand by those statements?" - Alice Stubbs, question during the deposition of Brad Cooper on October 2, 2008

Once Nancy's death was determined to be a homicide, Nancy's family sought custody of the Cooper children. As part of the custody case, Brad sat for a deposition on October 2, 2008. Considering the police's sole focus was on him for the murder of Nancy, Brad took a huge risk in agreeing to sit for a deposition. Alice Stubbs, a Raleigh attorney who drafted the Cooper's separation agreement, now represented Nancy's parents and sister. She conducted the questioning. Alice worked as a North Carolina judge prior to her work as a family law attorney.[ccvi] The media often referred to her as a "high-powered" Raleigh attorney, and she is apparently well-respected in Wake County.

Evaluating Brad's custody deposition provided detailed information into the lives of Nancy and Brad, but more importantly, it offered a window into Brad's thought processes and reactions to questions. The deposition provided hours of data on Brad's reactions, use of language, mannerisms, and other aspects of his syntax and speech delivery. The countless questions provide a baseline for how Brad answered questions and can be used to gauge stress and deception in his responses.

Clouding the vast benefits gained through the deposition was Alice Stubbs' performance. Alice has the tone and delivery usually reserved for conversations with toddlers. Yet at the same time, she was able to convey an air of condescension and arrogance while sounding as if she were speaking to a baby. Alice could not hide her shock and amazement at the details Brad was unable to provide. She failed to understand or even conceive of the weight of the situation surrounding Brad.

In early October, Brad was coping with the loss of his wife and children. The community and the police thought he killed his wife, and he had to remain professional in light of a woman asking him condescending questions in a small child's voice. Though he is one to conceal his emotions, at the time of the deposition, Brad was clearly under a tremendous amount of stress. Stress imposes many detrimental effects on a person's body and mind. It can affect one's memory and ability to think. Brad showed many signs of stress during the deposition.

Brad's brain may not work in the same manner as most, but the culmination of circumstances bearing down on him definitely exaggerated his natural attributes. During questioning, Brad could not remember his nephew's name, though he remembered it later in the day. He was unable to recall various names of co-workers at Cisco who were currently, as of October 2, 2008, on his team.[ccvii] Was he lying? What was the relevance of the questions and his inability to answer them? Though Alice openly displayed shock and disdain at Brad's inability to recall various events, many of his answers were irrelevant to his possible role in Nancy's death or to his regaining custody of his children.

Brad was not thinking clearly during the deposition. He attempted to answer the questions asked, but there were many instances where he could not recall things he should have been able to remember. There were other times where he simply did not know the answers, such as his inability to provide his mother's middle name or the year he graduated from college. These were two examples where most people would know the answers. It was quite unusual that Brad did not know these answers, but they were also telling as to how his mind works. He did not appear to retain certain information because he did not find it note-worthy, even if other people would. This comes into play when he does not remember facts that could have been important to the investigation of Nancy's death. However, at other times his memory was stellar. The details of Brad's memory had no discernable pattern and certainly did not correlate in a favorable manner for him.

During the deposition, Brad answered many questions in the present tense and utilized the pronoun, "we."[ccviii] When people are newly married, spouses often still use the pronoun *I* or *my* when *we* and *our* are more appropriate. It is a habit that can take years to break. Once a person has been married for some time, the transition to "we" takes hold. After the death of a spouse, often times the remaining spouse will continue to use *we* out of habit. Nonetheless, if a spouse murders his wife, the use of "we" and "us" often vanishes immediately. Many murdering husbands have been caught referring to their wife in the past tense when she was only missing. Further, the marital possessions, such as the house, quickly become *mine* not *ours*. Brad exhibited signs that he had not fully accepted Nancy's death at the time of his deposition (almost three months after her murder). Though some could argue Brad used *we* as a means to trick Alice, he instinctively utilized plural pronouns throughout the questioning.

Alice Stubbs undoubtedly entered this deposition with the belief Brad killed Nancy. It is hard to believe she would treat a man whose wife was just murdered with such disdain, unless she believed so. After Brad was unable to answer whether or not Nancy drank coffee before she ran, Alice responded in a condescending tone, "Did you live in the home with her?" She had no patience for any answers inconsistent with what she thought he should know.

Though the bar was set high for Brad's answers, the same cannot be said for Alice's preparation and interview skills. She failed to have maps available when she asked Brad about locations within Cary, North Carolina. She had Brad draw rudimentary maps, which were nowhere close to-scale. She did not have floor plans of the Cooper residence, even though she questioned Brad on the proximity of various aspects of his house. Alice also failed to review documents provided by Brad's attorneys prior to the deposition.[ccix]

Occasionally, Alice succinctly zeroed in on a key issue and delivered quality questions. Other times, she was all over the place and unable to remember what questions she had already asked. She asked Brad if he had reviewed the autopsy report from his dead wife and then followed by asking if he had a mortgage on his house. She also asked if Brad knew how many sports bras Nancy had.[ccx] This was a question that Nancy would have most likely not been able to answer accurately. What was the point of this question? What would have been the implication if Brad had attempted to answer this question? Alice's lack of interview skills distracted from the deposition throughout. At one point, she asked Brad, "Were you finished with your answer before your lawyer interrupted you?"[ccxi] Similar to the prosecutors in the criminal case, she could not keep her emotions out of the deposition.

She asked Brad to tell her exactly what Nancy said to him during a conversation. Giving Alice the benefit of the doubt, this question was designed to see how Brad reacted to a question where he could not answer it fully and accurately. Unless he taped the conversation, Brad would be unable to recall verbatim what Nancy said. As a result, his response would indicate hesitation and a little stress. If that was not her intent, it was a very poorly formed question.

Though the relevance to the custody case or even the murder investigation were not clear, Alice asked Brad about an affair he had with Heather Metour years prior. Brad openly admitted to the affair, though he provided very few details.[ccxii] This affair was also a central theme in the 2011 trial. Though Brad was not overly forthright regarding the affair, he admitted to it immediately, something that many people fail to do, since they are used to lying about an affair.

Regarding the affair with Heather, Alice asked Brad how many times he kissed her. Once again, this was a question that Brad would likely have no way of answering with any specificity. Many of Alice's questions would likely garner slightly different answers if asked multiple times. If Brad had provided a range or estimate, it would have likely been viewed as further deception. For example, if Brad had answered 15-25 times, but he had previously told an investigator he was not sure, then the police would have undoubtedly considered one or both of the statements as lies. The *authorities* in this case seemed completely unfamiliar with human response and the difference between variation and lying.

While working in budgeting and forecasting, I was often tasked with obtaining the sales projections from the various sales regional vice presidents. One thing I learned very quickly was that sales people did not like to work with numbers except when it came to calculating their commissions, and hated forecasting. If I asked a sales VP what her sales forecast was for next quarter or year, I would consistently receive an answer indicating she was not sure or had no idea. After numerous rounds of questions and possibly several meetings spanning weeks, I would eventually pin her down to a tight range and sometimes a specific number. Initially, she said she did not know, but later she agreed to a fairly precise number.

Was her first response a lie? She did change her answer. She did not know how much in sales bookings she would close the following period. Similar to Brad, she was also reluctant to provide an answer, as she knew there would be expectations associated with the answer. Usually, the primary factor holding her back was uncertainty. With regard to Brad, he genuinely did not know how many times he kissed Heather. He was also likely quite embarrassed to answer the question, especially if it was a lot. However, Brad knew any change to any answers he provided would be viewed as lies even if they were nuanced or slight modifications.

What caused the sales VP to go from not knowing to a precise number had to do with the manner in which I asked the questions. I also acknowledged the uncertainty. I knew the *precision* was not precise. Alice was asking Brad questions with the goal of tripping him up and possibly confusing him. Variation in his responses would not be seen as due to the uncertainty of actually knowing how many times he kissed Heather, but as a deliberate attempt at deception. Though the police and subsequently the prosecution viewed varying comments about his affair with Heather as deceptive, they had no bearing on his role, or lack of, in Nancy's death.

During the deposition, Alice asked the following question, "Tell me what you said about it [debt] in the affidavit."[ccxiii] What was the purpose of this question? To test his memory? Was she too lazy to read the affidavit, or was this just another poorly crafted question? Unfortunately for Brad, ill-conceived questions often led to misleading answers, for which no one gave him the benefit of the doubt.

The police seemed unable to correctly identify deception or misleading statements by Brad Cooper. The police also consistently zeroed in on irrelevant statements. They compared Brad's statements against those of Nancy's friends, and consistently believed the friends, even when they were not in a position to provide a reliable opinion. During the deposition, there were several questions that elicited stress and anxiety from Brad. There were deviations in Brad's responses that provided clues to where he was sensitive or managing answers, though the police failed to identify them.

Brad's potential affairs were an area of significant concern during the investigation and subsequent trial. Interestingly, no one seemed to apply the same logic to Nancy. Brad traveled to France as part of his master's in business administration (MBA) program. During his trip, there were rumors that Brad and a French student engaged in a sexual relationship. Attempting to better understand the relationship, the following exchange took place during the deposition:

> Alice Stubbs: Who is Celine Busson?

> Brad Cooper: Celine..um…Busson is a student of a French University…Ah...A university in France that my team at NC State College was paired up with. I was… We had a team here that teamed up with University members in class.[ccxiv]

Brad's response to the above question was different from how he answered other questions throughout the deposition. He hesitated more than his baseline. He changed his description of Celine mid-stream. He was not expecting this question. It stressed him. Moments later, the questioning cut straight to the point.

> Alice Stubbs: Did you spend the night with Celine Busson?

> Brad Cooper: No, I did not.

> Alice Stubbs: Did you sleep in the same room at any time with Celine Busson during that trip?

Brad Cooper: No, I did not.

Alice Stubbs: Did you kiss Celine Busson?

Brad Cooper: [pause] It is common in France to kiss each other on the cheek. Other than that, no.[ccxv]

The questions surrounding Celine clearly stressed Brad. He was not comfortable answering them, but he did. The first two responses he gave were direct and specific. With regard to the question of whether he kissed Celine, Brad clarified his answer. It appeared to be a legitimate clarification, but of the three questions, the one regarding kissing created a different response than the others. The possibility of an affair with Celine likely had no bearing on Nancy's death or the custody case. Other than establishing how Brad reacted to stressful questions, it provided no valuable information into Brad's guilt or innocence. It was not relevant unless he was still involved with her when Nancy was killed. Therefore, determining the status of the relationship could have been relevant.

Alice Stubbs: When is the last time you had contact with her [Celine Busson]?

Brad Cooper: To the best of my knowledge, give or take April, 2007. It could have been later, but as far as I remember it was April, 2007...give it a month or two. [ccxvi]

Through his response, Brad identified the limitations on his memory regarding contact with Celine. He openly admitted to a lack of confidence in his answer, or he provided an intentionally vague answer. If she was important to him, his memory may have been more concrete than he admitted. This would be especially true if he had recently communicated with her. If Brad had communicated with Celine in late 2007, it would have been outside of his estimate, but not to an unreasonable extent. If Brad had communicated with her in the last six months [March – October 2008 timeframe], then there would be reason to investigate further. However, no information had arisen to indicate this was the case.

The above examples provided indicators that Brad may have been stressed or was not being fully forthright with answers. However, we have an example during the deposition where we know the correct answer; therefore, we can assess how Brad reacted to a question he did not want to answer.

> Alice Stubbs: Were you able to access my emails to Nancy?
>
> Brad Cooper: Your emails to Nancy?
>
> Alice Stubbs: Um hum.
>
> Brad Cooper: If she sent any emails; it is not something I looked for. I am not too sure if she emailed you with the home account or not.[ccxvii]

Brad responded to the stressful question with a question. Often, people respond with a question to allow themselves time to think. If the questioner mumbled or asked a confusing question, responding with a question would be appropriate. Alice stated her question clearly. It was not confusing. Under these circumstances, it is usually a stall technique. Once Brad obtained his delay, he attempted to answer the question. He indicated, "…it is not something I looked for." This was a true statement, but it did not answer the question. People go to great lengths to not directly lie. Not answering the question is a common approach. He followed by saying he was not *too* sure… Brad utilized the word *too* to mean very or extremely. It qualified his answer. He may have been sure, but he was not *very* sure that Nancy sent Alice an email from her home account. Though not asked, Brad also specifically identified one of Nancy's email accounts. This tactic improved the accuracy of his statement, but moved him further away from the question asked. Brad was being evasive.

Brad set up Nancy's email account to send a copy of all emails coming and going to one of his email accounts.[ccxviii] Brad used it as an easy way to see what emails Nancy was sending and receiving. The prosecution utilized Brad's tactic as evidence of Brad's controlling nature. Though certainly an invasion of Nancy's privacy, it was a far cry from what many separating persons do, such as hiring a private investigator to follow their spouse. Since Brad reviewed Nancy's email, he saw one or more of her communications with her lawyer. As a result, this line of questioning provided a window into how Brad would respond when faced with admitting something that would make him look bad. The above pattern can be compared to answers he gave regarding Nancy's death. If Brad was concealing information, being deceptive, or hiding facts about Nancy's death, his responses should have been similar to the above format. They were not.

During the deposition, Brad was asked a series of questions related to cleaning his car. The obvious intent of this line of questioning was to ascertain whether or not Brad cleaned his car during the early morning hours of July 12. The questions alluded to the fact that Brad cleaned his car because he transported Nancy's dead body in his trunk.

Alice Stubbs: Did you vacuum your car on July 11, 2008?

Brad Cooper: No.

Alice Stubbs: Did you vacuum your car on July 12, 2008?

Brad Cooper: No.

Alice Stubbs: Did you vacuum it on the [July] thirteenth?

Brad Cooper: I don't believe I vacuumed it on the thirteenth, no.[ccxix]

The above questions dealt directly with the issue of Brad trying to cover-up the murder of Nancy. However, these answers differ greatly from the response Brad provided regarding reading Nancy's emails from her attorney. He did not ask a question with a question. There were no qualifying statements or caveats to his answers regarding whether or not he vacuumed his car on either July 11 or 12. Nothing in his responses conveyed any deception or stress. His answers were clear and direct. However, his response to the question for July 13 was different from the first two responses. Brad stated that he "didn't believe" he vacuumed, which indicated he was less confident in this answer. He also put *no* at the end of the response versus the beginning. Placing *no* at the end of a response can indicate distancing from an answer. It is a less direct way of denying an action or statement.

Based on Brad's responses, the most probable day he would have vacuumed his car was Sunday, July 13. Yet, it was quite improbable he vacuumed his car on Sunday. Most likely, he did not have a clear recollection of the day; thus, he demonstrated hesitancy in his answer. He was under tremendous stress on July 13. Regardless of Brad's involvement or lack of involvement in Nancy's death, the spotlight was clearly on Brad the day after Nancy went missing. People were observing his every move. If he had vacuumed the car on the thirteenth of July, one of his neighbors or friends, who were completely convinced he killed Nancy, would have reported it. In addition, the police were with Brad from the time they arrived at his house on July 12 until Nancy's body was found. He did not have an opportunity to clean his car on July 13. Brad's responses were absent signs of deception. He provided forthright answers to this line of questioning.

Another critical line of questioning during the deposition focused on the events of July 11 and 12. Brad's responses provide key indicators to his candor and forthrightness regarding what happened to Nancy.

Alice Stubbs: Did she [Nancy] run on July the twelfth?

Brad Cooper: Yes, she left the house at about 7:00 a.m.

Alice Stubbs: Did you go to sleep with them [his girls] on Friday the eleventh?

Brad Cooper: I did.

Alice Stubbs: What time would ya'all [sic] have fallen asleep?

Brad Cooper: The kids fell asleep about 9:00 p.m. I probably fell asleep soon after.

Alice Stubbs: Were you awakened at any time during the night?

Brad Cooper: When, when she [Nancy] opened the front door and I heard her come up the stairs, yeah, it woke me up.

Alice Stubbs: Did you get out of the bed?[ccxx]

Brad Cooper: I did not, no.

The case against Brad Cooper was predicated on Brad killing Nancy when she arrived home from the Duncan's party shortly after midnight. Brad's responses to the questions pertaining to this timeframe were direct and appeared to convey candor. However, Brad's answer regarding what time he fell asleep lacked the emphatic tone of the other answers. Brad responded that he "...*probably* fell asleep soon after."

Based on evidence later gathered from Brad's computer, he was on the Internet past 9:30 p.m. on the evening on July 11.[ccxxi]

Did he lie or forget that he was on the Internet after the girls went to sleep? It is not clear, but why would he lie unless he did something incriminating on the Internet? Instead, he visited various innocuous websites. It was more likely his hesitation in his response was a result of ambiguous memories regarding the time period in question than an attempt at intentional deception. Regardless, his response as to whether or not he got out of bed when Nancy came home was direct. He stayed in bed.

Brad's recollection regarding the events of the morning of July 12 was very elaborate. Brad conveyed details regarding where he was in the house when certain discussions or events took place. He explained where Bella, Katie, and Nancy were at various times throughout the morning. He answered those questions without hesitation, which would have been almost magical without the benefit of the memories. If he fabricated the information, he would have to think about it before he spoke. Even if he had already anticipated the question, he would have had to figure out how his current answer fit with previous answers he had given within the deposition and to the police. It would have been very easy, even for Alice, to confuse him if he were fabricating the details of the morning of July 12. In response to a question, Brad stated he opened the refrigerator door when Nancy asked him about the laundry. If he created this response from his imagination, as the police and prosecution believed, then he would have to remember the lie and to whom he told it. Otherwise, he could easily get confused when creating the scene during a separate interview.

Nancy was alive on the morning of July 12, prior to leaving the house for a run. There was no indication of deception from Brad's responses or statements regarding the morning of July 12. Coupled with the numerous eyewitnesses who saw her running later in the morning, Nancy was still alive at 7:00 a.m. on the morning of July 12.

Chapter 11 – If Not Brad…?

Brad's deposition provided hours of opportunity to assess Brad's character, thought processes, reactions to stress and most importantly, if he attempted to deceive the interviewer regarding Nancy's death. Though Brad did show signs of stress and apprehension around Nancy's email and Celine Busson, there was no indication of any deception regarding questions pertaining to Nancy's death. If Brad had done something to Nancy, he would have exhibited signs that he was misleading the interviewer, not fully answering the questions and hesitating before answering. He showed none of those indicators during key questions.

Nancy called Brad's cell phone at 6:40 a.m. on the morning of July 12, 2008. Based on a slew of witnesses, Nancy went running shortly after she made the call. She was killed during or after her run. While Brad was supposedly plotting and later covering-up her murder, he was casually surfing the Internet and checking emails. When Nancy was gone for too long, Brad called friends looking for her. He searched for her. On July 14, two days after Nancy went missing, Brad emailed her.[ccxxii] Brad acted in a manner which was consistent with someone believing Nancy was still alive, not someone who killed her.

The police completely botched the analysis of Brad's laptop by not validating the evidence found with even one of two possible sources. As a result, ambiguity remained around Brad's laptop. However, there was considerable evidence indicating tampering likely occurred. Someone seemingly planted temporary Internet files on Brad's computer. The evidence points away from Brad. If Brad did not kill Nancy, then who did?

Potential perpetrators of Nancy's murder range on the spectrum from complete strangers to immediate family. The rarest form of murder is one carried out by a complete stranger. This can be anything from a serial killer to road rage. It could also be a case of mistaken identity or a contract killing. Overall, stranger killings are rare and probably one of the hardest to solve as there is almost nothing tying the perpetrator to the victim other than the crime itself. There was little to indicate that Nancy was killed by a random psychopath who had no connection to her. There were no similar crimes before or since in the area, which negates a pattern consistent with a serial killer.

It was highly unlikely one or more homicidal maniacs plucked Nancy from a jogging path in broad daylight in the middle of Cary, North Carolina, one of the safest cities in the country. Though people reported suspicious vehicles in the area, there was nothing to indicate they had anything to do with Nancy's murder. If Nancy was taken by force while running and put into a vehicle, it was unlikely it would have occurred without noticeable bruising and scrapes on Nancy's body from the assault. The coroner did not find these types of injuries. There was nothing in the autopsy consistent with a struggle, which would have likely ensued from a stranger abduction while running.

For Nancy to have been abducted while running there would have been a vehicle parked on the side of the road or close to where she was taken. Since no one saw someone drag Nancy toward a van or load her into a truck, it does not bode well for a stranger abduction. It could have happened, but there was no evidence indicating a stranger abducted and killed Nancy.

The next rung is casual acquaintances. This could be someone who coveted Nancy from afar, saw her occasionally or a friend of a friend. Nancy was quite attractive and in great shape. She was also very outgoing and friendly. Nancy certainly had her share of admirers. If Nancy did not know the person or persons well, it was unlikely she would have willingly gotten into a vehicle with someone she barely knew, especially if she was in the middle of a run. This scenario still required someone to force her into a vehicle in broad daylight in a fairly populated area. It is also a remote possibility.

Closer in were Nancy's friends. Nancy had a strong, close-knit group of friends. They were all very supportive of her, and most of them seemed to completely adore her. Based on the erratic behavior of some of her friends during the investigation, a further review is warranted. One or more persons from the group may also fall into the following rung.

The final rung contained Nancy's immediate family and anyone with whom she had an intimate relationship. With Brad having been excluded and her girls of an age outside of consideration, Nancy's immediate family was quickly eliminated. Nancy's siblings and parents were out of the country when she was murdered, and there was no reasonable motive for them to kill her. This leads us to intimate relationships. Through almost no help from the Cary Police Department investigation, several potential paramours were identified. Nancy had two affairs early in her marriage to Brad; however, if the affairs ended well before her death, it was highly unlikely a former, stale lover killed her out of the blue. Regardless, recent or current relationships certainly warrant review. As with a spouse, boyfriends and lovers must be reviewed thoroughly. Passion can quickly turn negative under the wrong circumstances.

Prior to dating and marrying Brad, Nancy dated a man by the name of Brett Wilson.[ccxxiii] There was no indication that Nancy continued to see Brett after she married Brad. Yet, law enforcement found emails and phone records, which indicated that they reconnected shortly before her murder.[ccxxiv] Brett was located in Canada, and earlier in 2008 Nancy thought that she would be moving back to Canada. The reigniting of their relationship was likely predicated on Nancy completing the move north. With those plans having been cancelled, or at least postponed, there was no indication they met any time in 2008. As a result, with Brett Wilson in Canada and their relationship likely consisting only of electronic communication, he was not in a position to be reasonably considered, even as a person of interest, in Nancy's death.

In October of 2005, Nancy had an affair with a man from the Lochmere neighborhood, John Pearson.[ccxxv] John Pearson was married to Kinde Pearson. While married to Kinde, he also had an affair with Heather Metour. *Yes, the same woman who had an affair with Brad.* As a result of the affair, Kinde sued Heather for alienation of affection, which is a law in North Carolina that allows a spouse to sue an individual who caused a married person to lose the affection of their spouse. In May of 2008, Nancy called John Pearson to ask about the lawsuit. Based on Mr. Pearson's testimony, he was skeptical of Nancy's call and asked to meet her in a public place. When they got together, Nancy discussed the lawsuit with John as well as possibly trying to get him to persuade Heather to testify against Brad during the Cooper's upcoming divorce.[ccxxvi] Though Nancy mentioned the two of them running together in the future, there were no other indications of a resurgence in their relationship.

After Nancy's murder, Mr. Pearson came to the attention of the police. In August of 2008, Detective Adam Dismukes of the Cary Police Department interviewed John Pearson. Mr. Pearson was someone who was familiar with both Nancy and Brad Cooper. Previously, he ran in similar social circles when he lived in the Lochmere area. Mr. Pearson answered questions pertaining to his relationship with both Brad and Nancy. He provided general and specific information about the Coopers. However, Mr. Pearson left out a key piece of information during his first interview with the police. He failed to mention that he had sex with Nancy three years prior. His lie was one of omission. When the defense attorney asked about the truthfulness of his statements during this interview, he stated:

John Pearson: I thought that I answered his questions completely ...honestly. I excluded like I said earlier that one night uh where Nancy and I went back to her house on Halloween in 2005. It was three years earlier. I did not include that in my first interview. Once asked about it in a

second interview, I addressed it
completely, thoroughly.[ccxxvii]

Though Mr. Pearson did not want to look badly in the
courtroom, his response called into question his candor
within the investigation. He indicated that he answered the
questions "completely" and "honestly," yet he omitted a
potentially defining aspect of his relationship with Nancy.
He attempted to present his second interview as the time he
came clean about his relationship with Nancy, but he was far
from overly candid. He did not *offer* the information
regarding his relationship with Nancy; he was directly asked
about it. Many people omit information as an attempt not to
lie, though on some level they are aware of their deceptive
tactic. Mr. Pearson was not willing to acknowledge the
deceptive element of his first interview with the police.

In September of 2008, Detective Dismukes interviewed Mr.
Pearson a second time. Based on the initial questions, the
purpose of the interview was to ask follow-up questions
regarding his relationship with Nancy. The police learned
that Mr. Pearson may have been romantically interested in
Nancy. He was asked if he ever had a crush on Nancy. Mr.
Pearson said, "No." He also indicated that there was
nothing romantic between him and Nancy, but then went on
to admit they engaged in sexual activity in October of 2005.[ccxxviii]
He initially stated that, "Nancy and I got a little physical."[ccxxix]
He did everything he could to downplay the incident. He
referred to the interaction as "making out on the couch," but
later said they could have had intercourse.[ccxxx]

At one point during his second interview, Mr. Pearson made
a very odd statement when referring to the secrecy of their

affair. He implied it was more Nancy's secret because he was already getting divorced at the time. When Detective Dismukes asked him about it, he answered the question with a question. Then Mr. Pearson said that he had not considered getting divorced at that time.[ccxxxi] Mr. Pearson's statements were not clear on the audio tape interview, but he appeared to be trying to mislead Detective Dismukes about the state of his marriage at that time.

Notwithstanding Mr. Pearson's diversionary statements, as Detective Dismukes asked clarifying questions he was forced to acknowledge the contrary. Many of Mr. Pearson's statements conveyed a considerable comfort when he was omitting facts, failing to answer questions and insinuating things that were likely not true.

During the second interview, the topic of a rumor about John Pearson surfaced. The following exchange took place:

> Detective Dismukes: What was the negative rumor Nancy told Scott Heider [about John Pearson]? What was that?

> John Pearson: He [Scott Heider] said something about that…I confronted Nancy on it… First of all, why are you [Nancy] saying negative things about me?[ccxxxii]

Mr. Pearson never answered the question, which was an indicator of stress. Later, Detective Dismukes circled back to the question again and this time Mr. Pearson answered, "I can't remember what she said," though he did remember what she said during the trial two and a half years after the interview. The rumor involved John Pearson having feelings for Nancy.[ccxxxiii]

Mr. Pearson referred to the statement made by Scott Heider as "negative." He also referred to it as a "rumor," which implied it was not true. In his initial response, Mr. Pearson indicated that he asked Nancy why she said negative things about him. However, if he believed it was not true, then why did his response not convey that? He did not ask Nancy, "Why are you saying untrue things about me?" Since he failed to clarify the truthfulness of Nancy's statement when he referred to the conversation with her, there was likely some truth to the rumor. Mr. Pearson admitted to sexual activity with Nancy, but he denied having any feelings for her. Furthermore, why did he consider having feelings for her as such a *negative* thing? What was John Pearson not telling the police?

During the second interview, Mr. Pearson clearly told Detective Dismukes that he knew Nancy's running routes.[ccxxxiv] He also testified during the trial that he exercised with Nancy.[ccxxxv] Nevertheless, when a defense attorney asked Mr. Pearson about his statements regarding Nancy's running routes, he said he misspoke during the interview. He said his answer was misleading. He did not know Nancy's running routes. He said he was familiar with the area where she ran, and his answer reflected his guess as to where he would have run if he lived where Nancy did.[ccxxxvi] Unfortunately, the statements he made during the interview were not consistent with his new interpretation of the conversation. After he tried to clarify his statements, the following exchange took place during the trial:

Defense attorney: You never ran with her [Nancy]?

John Pearson: "I never ran with her. I never saw her running."ccxxxvii

He ended his response with a comment regarding not having seen Nancy run. Mr. Pearson was clearly attempting to deny having anything to do with Nancy's disappearance, even though he was not directly asked. During the second interview with the police, he was rightfully concerned about becoming a suspect.

In the second interview, Mr. Pearson had to clarify, retract, and change several statements he had made. He showed signs that he was concerned about what his changing statement meant for him. He down-played his relationship with Nancy as much as he could, diverted the police toward another potential suspect, acknowledged feelings of remorse, provided theories on how she disappeared, and openly fished for information regarding how he fit into the investigation. Mr. Pearson was quite nervous during the second interview.

Mr. Pearson likely believed the idea of having feelings for Nancy could be considered a motive by the police. He did not want to become a potential suspect in Nancy's murder. At the time of the second interview, Brad had not been arrested. Mr. Pearson was not in the tight circle of friends who were being fed daily information by the police. Mr. Pearson was very concerned. If he admitted to having romantic feelings for Nancy or if there were rumors of such, he had to shut them down immediately. Whether it was the truth or a version of the truth he decided to adopt, his relationship with Nancy was nothing more than a one-night fling. Though he was vague about many things, he did not waver on this fact.

Mr. Pearson also directed the police toward an alternative person of interest, "Michael." Michael worked out at the gym with Nancy and went to her pool. He said the man acted strangely toward Nancy, but he did not provide any specifics.[ccxxxviii] He conveyed no articulable facts that substantiated his concern. Without overtly stating it, he alluded to many things about Michael. He insinuated that he may have had a relationship with Nancy. He also indicated that it was a long-shot.[ccxxxix] Regardless, he pointed the police in his direction.

During Mr. Pearson's second interview with Detective Dismukes, he made an indirect, quasi-admission. He stated twice during the interview that he felt guilty regarding Nancy.[ccxl] He implied it was a result of his sexual indiscretions, but the connection was not obvious. He also made the disturbing statement, "I never meant to hurt her [Nancy] at all, as far as saying anything negative about her."[ccxli] His statements were eerily close to admissions regarding Nancy's death. Mr. Pearson had stress and guilt regarding Nancy. It was not clear from where exactly these feelings stemmed.

Mr. Pearson also managed to convey his theory on what happened to Nancy. He told Detective Dismukes that he thought Nancy went running with someone she was having an affair with who no one else knew about.[ccxlii] It was certainly a plausible theory based on his knowledge of Nancy's *extra-curricular* activities. Alternatively, Mr.

Pearson could have been inadvertently talking about himself. Depending on which of his statements were true, Mr. Pearson had gone running with Nancy previously. He was also someone she had an affair with, although no one else knew about it at the time. Based on the fact he likely had his children with him on the morning of July 12, he probably did not go running with Nancy on the morning of her disappearance, but it certainly should have been investigated further. Interestingly, it was roughly the same alibi Brad had regarding watching his children.

The final noteworthy component of Mr. Pearson's interview was his concern and questions regarding his role in the investigation. He asked if he would be interviewed again. He openly expressed concern that he may not provide the exact same story if he were asked similar but not exact questions at a different time. Though memories are not precise and variances do occur, why was he so concerned about changes to his story? Was he worried he would not remember what he said during this interview? If his statements were the truth, he should not have been concerned. Regardless, Detective Dismukes brushed this concern aside. As the interview was coming to a close, Mr. Pearson's stress levels appeared to rise as he kept circling back to his role within the investigation. He was fishing for information. He wanted to know if Detective Dismukes thought he warranted a closer look.[ccxliii] Detective Dismukes never directly answered his round-about question, but he revealed his answer by not following-up with Mr. Pearson.

Mr. Pearson offered several reasons for why he failed to tell the police about the affair during his first interview. He stated that it was not relevant to the investigation. He said he wanted to spare any embarrassment for his ex-wife and children. Mr. Pearson also mentioned that he believed his affair with Nancy could adversely impact his professional reputation.[ccxliv] All the reasons he provided were certainly believable, but the change in his story should have caused Detective Dismukes some concern. Many people lie about affairs. It occurred several years before Nancy's murder, but it still should have been investigated thoroughly. Mr. Pearson's changed story and deliberate deception of the police did not draw the same reaction as any of Brad's supposed deceptions.

The Cary Police Department failed to establish if Mr. Pearson had an alibi for the early morning hours of July 12, when Nancy went missing. Even though Mr. Pearson offered his ex-wife's timecard for July 12 as some semblance of an alibi, Detective Dismukes did not take it.[ccxlv] It was not clear what the timecard would have proven. They did not ask him for phone records. They never asked to search his house or for him to provide a DNA sample. The police failed to fully corroborate information he told them. And the police failed to interview him again after he had admitted to a sexual relationship with the deceased.

John Pearson started having an affair with Heather Metour in May or June of 2005. Just prior, Brad also had an affair with Heather Metour. John Pearson had a supposed one-time affair with Nancy in the fall of 2005. John Pearson admitted to these two affairs, but we do not know if he had additional affairs. He was not specifically asked, and he demonstrated a propensity to selectively determine what the police should and should not know. We also do not know who else Heather was sleeping with, or who else may have been involved in the apparent complex and over-lapping sexual web in the Lochmere area. The police never attempted to understand or unravel the various sexual relationships engulfing this case, even though it may well have had everything to do with Nancy's unfortunate demise.

Though it was supposedly a secret, by sleeping with John Pearson Nancy could have angered at least two women: John's wife at the time, Kinde, and John's on-again, off-again paramour, Heather Metour. If John was sleeping with one or more other women, they could have been angry or jealous of Nancy as well.

There was speculation that Nancy may have also been sleeping with one or more other men. If one or more of these men were in other relationships, there was potential for other women to have been furious with Nancy. Or, one of the men vying for Nancy's affections may have felt rage toward Nancy as a result of jealousy or because he was rebuffed. Since the police failed to aggressively pursue any of these angles we have little to pursue other than speculation. However, Mr. Pearson provided statements that can be evaluated, and many of them warranted further investigative actions.

Mr. Pearson claimed he spent July 11, 2008 with Heather Metour. He left her house around 6:30 a.m. on the morning of July 12. Based on his statements, he had his kids with him during the morning and early afternoon. However, where was Heather during this time? Though Nancy wanted to use Heather in her upcoming divorce proceedings, how did she feel about Nancy? Did she have hostility toward her? It is an unknown.

According to John, both he and Heather Metour looked for Nancy on Sunday, July 13. Though it could have been staged, people do not usually make significant efforts to look for someone they know is already dead. Even though the likelihood of John or Heather having been involved in Nancy's death is low, it should have been investigated thoroughly.

There were allegations Nancy had other potentially intimate relationships. Apparently, one of Nancy's friends, Michelle Simmons, thought Nancy's relationship with her husband Tim was inappropriate.[ccxlvi] There were possibly other relationships we do not know about, since other individuals did not willingly come forward. Limited information was gathered on the accuracy of the allegations. Only months before her death, Nancy alluded to an intimate relationship with someone by the name of "Brett." She claimed it was Brett Wilson from Canada, but more than one of her friends may have thought it was Brett Adam, including Brett's wife, Jessica Adam, the woman who made the call to the police reporting Nancy missing.

Chapter 12 – "I had a bad feeling..."

From Nancy's disappearance to the conviction of Brad Cooper for her murder, the case started and ended with Jessica Adam. She set the law enforcement wheels in motion by calling the Cary Police Department less than seven hours after Nancy left her house. Jessica influenced the neighbors and friends gathered outside of the Cooper residence on July 12 by pointing the blame directly toward Brad. At this point, Nancy had merely not returned home within a reasonable period of time from when she was expected. Nancy was not known for her promptness, and it would not have been the first time she changed plans without telling others. Though her absence was troubling by the early afternoon, it was still explainable. Assigning blame was a little premature when no one other than the killer and whomever he may have told knew what happened to Nancy. Later, the police utilized extensive information provided by Jessica to develop affidavits for search warrants. Jessica gave the police the basis for a struggle in the foyer of the Cooper home. She attempted to discredit Brad's trips to Harris Teeter on the morning Nancy went missing. The police viewed Jessica as a concerned, unbiased source of information, who also happened to validate what they were already thinking.

Jessica and her husband Brett moved to Cary, North Carolina in 2006. They have two children. Prior to living in North Carolina, they lived in California.[ccxlvii] Jessica met Nancy in June of 2006 when they both showed up a day early for pre-school.[ccxlviii] They became fast friends.

Jessica was a pivotal person within the police investigation. She provided key pieces of information and seemed to be guiding the investigation throughout. Though much of the information she provided was wrong and misleading, the police did not seem to care. Incriminating Brad was much more important to the police than ensuring the complete accuracy of the information she provided. As Jessica *clarified* her statements, the police simply adjusted their focus as the information changed.

According to Jessica, she was in near constant contact with Nancy on the eve of her disappearance. During Jessica's 2011 trial testimony, the following exchange took place:

> Prosecutor: Did you speak to her [Nancy] on that Friday, July eleventh?
>
> Jessica Adam: Yes, I did.
>
> Prosecutor: Did you speak to her in the morning [of July 11]?
>
> Jessica Adam: I would have spoken to her at some point that morning.[ccxlix]

Jessica's response to the first question was direct and concise. However, when asked if she spoke to Nancy on the morning of July 11, her response was much less direct. Jessica stated she "would have" spoken to Nancy. *Would have* is not the past tense of speak; *spoke* is. *Would have* is used with *if* or other similar phrasing that conveys something that did not happen. For example, "I would have spoken to her, *if* I saw her." Based on Jessica's word selection, she likely did not speak to Nancy on the morning of July 11. This conclusion was further validated by Jessica's use of the vague phrase "at some point" when referring to when she spoke to Nancy. Jessica likely spoke to Nancy, but it was not in the morning.

Supposedly, the purpose of the morning call was for Jessica and Nancy to coordinate Jessica's visit to the Cooper house later in the day. Jessica was to help Nancy organize and clean her house in exchange for Nancy's painting the dining room in the Adam's house.[ccl] In the late afternoon, Jessica claimed she visited the Cooper residence.[ccli] Jessica initially told the police she spoke to Nancy on the phone on the afternoon of July 11, though she later changed her story to incorporate an in-person trip to the Cooper home. This change in her story did not cause the police any concern. During this supposed visit, Jessica walked through the house in order to get ideas for how she could help Nancy organize. They also discussed plans for the weekend. According to Jessica, Nancy planned to visit Jessica's house the following morning at 8:00 a.m. to paint the dining room, while Jessica would go to Nancy's on Sunday to organize.[cclii]

Some people questioned Jessica's assertions regarding plans for Nancy to paint at her house on the morning of July 12. Nonetheless, Jessica had a corroborating source for her claims. Carey Clark, who was supposed to run with Nancy on the morning of July 11, told the Cary Police Department that Nancy told her about the plans to paint on Saturday morning.[ccliii]

Unfortunately, Carey's story did not line up with what Jessica had told the police. According to Jessica, she and

Nancy made the Saturday plans to paint during the late afternoon of July 11, while Carey claimed Nancy told her about the painting plans at 5:20 a.m., approximately 12 hours prior to when the plans were supposedly made.[ccliv] Carey also claimed she and Nancy had made plans to run Sunday morning, which contradicted Jessica's other claim that she was going to clean and organize Nancy's house on Sunday morning.[cclv] Though Carey was supposed to have been corroborating Jessica's claims, her statements directly contradicted Jessica's assertions.

With Jessica's supposed in-person visit to the Cooper residence on July 11, an entirely new line of incriminating evidence opened up against Brad. Since Jessica was present in the Cooper house the day before Nancy disappeared, she was in a position to compare pictures the police took of the house from the afternoon of July 12 to what she saw the preceding afternoon. Jessica identified several items throughout the house that had changed from the day prior. She told the police that items had been removed from the foyer.[cclvi] There were wooden ducks present the previous day, but they were mysteriously missing from the pictures she reviewed. There were decorative sticks missing, and a rug, which was in the foyer the day prior, was now laid out flat in the playroom.[cclvii]

Suddenly, Jessica's presence on July 11 provided a treasure trove of information to the police on how much the house had changed during the period when Nancy went missing. The police took the information Jessica provided them and crafted a scenario. Missing and moved items were evidence of a struggle between Brad and Nancy in the foyer.

The police and prosecutors clung to Jessica's every word, though many of her statements were later found to be incorrect. The ducks were not in the foyer area on July 11 as Jessica had claimed. Brad's mother, Carol Cooper, testified that she found two of the ducks packed in boxes in the Cooper house weeks after Nancy's murder. The third duck was sitting on top of the refrigerator. In an apparent slip of the tongue, prosecutor Howard Cummings responded to the revelation that the ducks were clearly not in the foyer on July 11 by stating that this information "...make(s) them [witnesses for the State] look like a bunch of liars."[cclviii] Jessica definitely fell into this group. Did Jessica actually visit the Cooper household on July 11? If not, she was misleading the police with the intent of incriminating Brad.

At the end of Jessica's supposed visit to the Cooper residence, she and Nancy discussed their plans for the weekend. During this meeting they supposedly agreed that Nancy would paint the following morning. Jessica was asked about this conversation during her trial testimony:

Prosecutor: Did you discuss with her [Nancy] that afternoon when she was going to paint your dining room?

Jessica Adam: We did. Ah, before [sic] shortly before I left we confirmed plans for me to come back to her house on that Sunday to organize. That was why I was walking through to see if there was anything I needed to go purchase at the store. Ah, then we also, she then said to me (eyes closed), why don't I come (clears throat)

first thing tomorrow morning, 8 o'clock,
at your house and paint the dining room.

The question did not specify whether or not the conversation took place at the Cooper house, but it was implied. Jessica answered, "We did." This direct response indicated that she and Nancy did discuss painting her dining room on the afternoon of July 11. She stumbled through the rest of her response, which could indicate stress and/or a lack of certainty in her statements. As with the call to the police, Jessica felt compelled to further explain her actions. She was not confident in her assertions and felt she needed to justify why she was at Nancy's house. When Jessica began addressing the specifics of the plan, her stress level seemed to increase significantly.

When Jessica mentioned Nancy's comments to her, she closed her eyes. When someone closes her eyes it can often be a distancing maneuver. The individual detaches from what she is saying and disassociates from the words by closing her eyes. Jessica then cleared her throat in the middle of her recitation of Nancy's supposed comments, which can also indicate stress. She ended the statement by saying, "…why don't I [Nancy] come first thing tomorrow morning, 8 o'clock, at your house and paint the dining room." Since people do almost anything to avoid directly lying, they will leave words out and imply truth, even though the statements do not actually convey the complete truth. Upon first reading, Jessica's statement seemed to indicate that Nancy said she would come over to Jessica's house at 8:00 a.m. the next morning. However, upon dissecting her statement, she does not say that at all. Not only did Jessica leave words out of her statement, but she put the phrases in the wrong order. The first portion of her statement should have said that Nancy would come over to her house tomorrow morning. What she actually said was, "why don't I come first thing." It did not state where she was going. It was also in the form of a question, which was less definitive. Jessica then stopped her statement abruptly and said, "8 o'clock." She did not say *at* 8 o'clock. She merely stated a time. She followed the time with the phrase, "at your house and paint the dining room." This phrase was separate from the time and from Nancy going to Jessica's house the following morning. There were three separate statements awkwardly linked together as one thought. Nancy was going somewhere the following morning. She may have mentioned the time 8 o'clock, but most likely not in relation to their painting plans. Further, "at your house" was completely separate from the other portions of the statement. She distanced it from the time and date. It is likely that Nancy was going to paint the dining room, but not the following morning at 8 o'clock.

Later, on the evening of July 11, Jessica and her friend Mary Anderson were relaxing at Jessica's house having a glass of wine. Jessica called Nancy and invited her over. Nancy indicated that she had enough to drink and she was staying at the Duncan's house.[cclix] Jessica provided a fairly elaborate breakdown of what she and Nancy talked about during this call. Though she was not asked, Jessica felt compelled to address the possibility that painting plans were cancelled during the call. She stated, "I didn't, she didn't cancel any plans with me... It was still my understanding she was coming in the morning."[cclx] Based on the level of detail Jessica provided, the call likely occurred, but it was not evident whether or not plans were in fact cancelled during the call.

Even though Nancy was supposedly coming over the following morning at 8:00 a.m., Jessica's actions seemed to suggest otherwise. When asked what she needed to do in order to have the room ready for Nancy to paint, Jessica responded, "Well I, that morning, um it was 8 o'clock and maybe a minute or two after and I jumped out of bed and asked my husband to join me in clearing the dining room of its furniture... He got up."[cclxi] Jessica expected Nancy to arrive at her house at 8:00 a.m., yet she failed to awake until after the agreed-upon time. In addition, though she indicated she was not looking forward to waking early on a Saturday morning, she waited until the morning to move the furniture, which required her to awaken even earlier.

Continuing with the line of questioning, one of the prosecutors asked Jessica to expand on what she did on the morning of July 12. Jessica responded, "As I said, my husband and I cleared the dining room...At some point I started, I called her on her cell phone, at some point that morning. That was the first place I tried her. I remember trying her on her cell phone and getting no answer."[cclxii] Though the prosecutor's question did not specifically ask if Jessica tried to call Nancy, she addressed it. She stated she called Nancy's cell phone. However, she never used Nancy's name during the response. She used the pronoun "her" five times. Pronouns are an acceptable means for referring to a person, but most people still utilize the person's name at some point. Otherwise, the reference is too vague and indirect. Jessica likely failed to utilize Nancy's name because it allowed her to make a technically correct statement. She never said she called Nancy's cell phone, she said she called *her* cell phone. Allegedly, there was no record of Jessica calling Nancy's cell phone on the morning of July 12. If that was the case, Jessica's statement was a fabrication.[cclxiii] Unlike Brad's confusion over the dress Nancy wore on July 11 or discrepancies regarding where he cleaned, Jessica's statement was potentially critical to Nancy's death.

According to sources who have viewed the cell phone records, Jessica did not call Nancy on her cell phone on July 12.[cclxiv] She was so concerned about Nancy's whereabouts that she called friends and neighbors. She reported Nancy's disappearance to the police, but she never once called Nancy's cell phone. Jessica did not want this minor detail to come to anyone's attention. She did not have a good explanation for why she never attempted to contact Nancy directly through the most likely means. The police never questioned Jessica regarding her actions surrounding Nancy's disappearance. She was seen as a helpful friend and ally. Regardless, Jessica managed to trip herself up through her revealing responses.

Though Jessica claimed she and her husband got out of bed a little after 8:00 a.m., according to Brett, Jessica got him out of bed at 7:00 a.m.[cclxv] He did not stipulate whether Jessica was already out of bed when she woke him or if she got up at the same time as he did.[cclxvi] It was not immediately apparent whose version of what time the couple awoke was the correct one. Jessica was a quasi-reliable source who had been proven incorrect many times during the trial. Her statements were almost all geared toward making Brad look guilty. As a result, Brett seemed more credible. If his version was correct, what did Jessica and Brett do between

7:00 a.m. and 8:45 a.m., when Jessica claimed they had breakfast? Around 9:30 a.m., Jessica called the Cooper home phone the one and only time during the day.[cclxvii] Jessica supposedly expected Nancy at 8:00 a.m., but she did not try to contact her for an hour and a half.

After calling the Cooper house and speaking to Brad, Jessica went to the gym with her friend Mary Anderson.[cclxviii] While at the gym, she asked Hannah Prichard's husband if he had seen Nancy.[cclxix] After returning home from the gym, Jessica called Diana Duncan asking if she had seen Nancy, though she conveyed it more as, "Nancy seems to be missing."[cclxx] Under the guise of looking for Nancy, Jessica was spreading the word that Nancy was missing.

Around 1:30 p.m., Brad called Jessica to get Cary Clark's phone number. During the call, Jessica also got Hannah Prichard's phone number from Brad. Brad told Jessica he was putting the girls in the car and heading out to look for Nancy. Jessica then called Hannah.[cclxxi] After speaking to Hannah, Jessica decided it was time to get the police involved.

At just after 1:50 p.m. on the afternoon of July 12, 2008, Jessica called the non-emergency line of the Cary Police Department to report Nancy missing.[cclxxii] *To listen to the call in its entirety, please go to:* *https://www.youtube.com/watch?v=2gsAphXAuvA.* It was by no means what would have been expected from a call of this nature. The call lasted almost ten minutes. Jessica delivered many diatribes and tangents off the topic at hand. Though the call seemed highly disorganized, Jessica likely thought through what she was going to say prior to making the call.

She decided a call needed to be made. She looked up the non-emergency number. She also needed to make sure she conveyed the right information to the police in order to *find* Nancy.

There were many peculiar things about the call. Jessica began the call by indicating her friend had been missing since 7:00 a.m. without providing her friend's name. She immediately referenced the fact that her missing friend was in the middle of a divorce, though the Coopers were not in the process of divorcing. She added to the comment by saying "...because of the situation with the divorce...", but she failed to address what the 'situation' was.[cclxxiii] Why did Jessica feel the need to mention divorce twice prior to even identifying Nancy as the missing person in question? Her initial opening statement to the operator exceeded 150 words, but she failed to identify Nancy Cooper by name. For some reason, Jessica felt it was more important for the police to know about the divorce than who was actually missing.

Jessica used the phrase "you know" eight times during the call. "You know" is considered filler. It is a common phrase used in our culture, even by intelligent and articulate people. It is a phrase used subconsciously for several reasons with the most likely reason being nervousness.[cclxxiv] When people are uncertain of what to say, "you know" and "uh" can fill the space. It can also signal deception as the person is nervous or hesitant because she is attempting to mislead.[cclxxv] Jessica definitely seemed nervous during the non-emergency call to the police. The important question was why?

Well into the call, the operator asked Jessica for the name and address of her missing friend. Jessica provided the answers and then returned to the topic of the divorce. She added that Brad and Nancy were living together, but they were going through a divorce. The operator asked Jessica if she had tried to contact Nancy. Jessica did not answer this question. She did not want to answer the question, since she had not attempted to directly contact Nancy. The answer was no. Earlier, Jessica called the Cooper home, which enabled her to reach Brad. Why did Jessica call the home phone line, a number she rarely utilized, instead of calling Nancy on her cell phone? Jessica knew if she answered the question it would have discredited her entire call.

As Jessica continued, she indicated that Nancy should have been at her house "...no later than 9 o'clock." What Jessica actually said was, "She she [sic] should have been here. She was expected here..."[cclxxvi] Jessica did not say, "I was expecting her," or "I was expecting Nancy." Was Jessica not expecting her? She utilized passive language to create distance between herself and Nancy coming over. Jessica also used the pronoun "she" twice in a row, which illustrated stress around her mentioning Nancy's name.

Earlier in the call, Jessica stated she expected Nancy at her house at 8:00 a.m., but now she indicated Nancy should have been there by 9:00 a.m. Why the change in time? Jessica's statement implied the 8:00 a.m. time was not a firm commitment. She also strangely utilized formal language ("no later than") in the middle of ramblings, stuttering, and heavy breathing. The change in language was a marked inconsistency from other portions of the call, which reduces the reliability of this statement. The overall structure of her response could indicate Jessica was being less than forthright with this statement.

Jessica continued by conveying her thoughts regarding Brad's role in Nancy's disappearance. She tried to validate her theory by adding the complimentary opinion of another one of Nancy's friends, Hannah Prichard. Hannah was also concerned Nancy's husband did something to her. Since Hannah had the same thoughts, it added weight to Jessica's claims. In reality, it seemed Jessica suggested the concern to Hannah rather than Hannah coming to the conclusion independently.[cclxxvii]

Picking up on the repeated comments about Nancy's husband, the operator asked a question that Jessica was unprepared to answer: had he been violent with her in the past? Based on the discussion thus far, the operator likely figured the answer was yes. However, Jessica could not answer yes to this question as much as she wanted to. She responded, "Well, we, we, I don't [sic] he is definitely um been uh…"[cclxxviii] She stammered with her answer and used inconsistent verb tense demonstrating the stress this question caused her. Jessica also slipped in the phrase "he is definitely" into the middle of her response. If one only heard that portion of her response, he would think she was getting ready to say Brad was definitely violent. Nonetheless, Jessica did not finish her thought. She could not overtly lie, but she had to continue to perpetrate her goal of pointing the police toward Brad.

After the initial part of her response, Jessica cleared her throat, one of only two times during the entire call. She also cleared her throat again during this same response. With a few exceptions, one clears her throat when stressed or not confident in her statement. The question clearly rattled Jessica. If Jessica had been clearing her throat throughout the call, then it could be attributed to nerves, allergies, or just excessive talking, but she did not. She only cleared her throat when asked about Brad's violence. Jessica tried very hard to convey to the police operator that Nancy's husband was responsible for what happened to Nancy, yet this question cut through all of her prepared comments. At this point Nancy was only missing.

Her response continued with, "I don't know that he's been physically violent..."[cclxxix] Prior to this statement, Jessica had not-so-subtly told the operator Brad was responsible for Nancy's disappearance. Now, she shifted to the stance that she could not verify the violence, but it still could have happened. The burden was on the husband to prove he had not been violent. Next, Jessica stated, "There's been a lot of tension and uh [sic] so I wouldn't be surprised. I hate to say it..."[cclxxx] She equated tension with violence and then reduced her strong statement to nothing more than suggesting that if violence did take place, it would not have surprised her. The accusatory nature of her statements shifted to the hypothetical realm. As if the operator adopted Jessica's most recent logical concept, she asked if it was *possible* Nancy forgot she was supposed to be at Jessica's or did something else. She conceded the possibility, but then provided some rather confusing information. Jessica stated that Nancy's car was, "...parked in the driveway at home and her cell phone is there."[cclxxxi]

Throughout the call, Jessica appeared concerned that the operator did not believe her. She lacked confidence in what she said. Her story was not convincing. Out of desperation, Jessica's utterance was detailed and quite revealing. She could have easily stated that Nancy did not have her cell phone with her, or Nancy's phone was at her home. Jessica's concern must have been that her comment would prompt more questions than answers. Instead, she provided a very detailed description with a lot of unnecessary words for such a short statement. Unnecessary words are often indicative of deception as the person nervously adds unneeded words to convey the information.[cclxxxii]

Nancy's car was "parked" in the driveway. *Parked* was an unnecessary word. Nancy's car was in the driveway sufficiently provided the same information. Jessica also added "at home." With *at home* the use of driveway was not needed. Nancy's car could have been in the garage or on the street, but it did not matter. Jessica provided unnecessary words that provided additional information beyond what she wanted to convey.

Why *parked*? If Nancy's cell phone was in her car, but her car was not parked, then it was possible, even likely, Nancy had driven her car somewhere. This was not consistent with Jessica's message of oddities surrounding her inability to locate Nancy. The benefit of identifying where Nancy's car was parked (on the driveway) potentially eliminated the question of how Jessica knew the cell phone was in her car if the car was in the garage. Regardless, the words appeared meaningless though they provided a good deal of useful information about what Jessica may have done prior to the call.

Jessica took the long way to convey a simple point: Nancy did not have her cell phone with her. However, the more important question regarding her statement was how did Jessica know Nancy's phone was in her car at home? Brad could have told her the location of Nancy's phone. This was certainly a possibility, though she did not reference Brad. When Jessica mentioned statements from Brad she downplayed their accuracy, yet she wanted to emphasize this information. She wanted the operator to know Nancy did not have her phone because she thought that added weight to her claims of strangeness surrounding Nancy's disappearance.

If Brad did not tell Jessica the location of Nancy's phone, she may have fabricated the statement to validate the point she was making; Nancy is missing; you should look at her husband very closely. If so, it meant she intentionally deceived the police. She believed it was so important for the police to take her seriously that it justified her telling one little distortion of the truth. Her statement may have been true, but she could not validate it. Jessica utilized the call to lead the police toward a goal. The police needed to suspect Brad of wrong-doing. Interestingly, nothing else Jessica said on the call was an outright lie. She may have misled the police with insinuations she could not support, but it all fell *technically* outside the sphere of a direct lie. Her comments and responses were in the realm of truth. The statement Nancy's phone was in her car would have been her first blatant lie, which was inconsistent with the rest of the call. Jessica likely did not overtly lie with this statement; she may have just withheld a little of the truth.

Jessica could have driven over to the Cooper residence prior to making the call to the police. This would explain how Jessica knew that Nancy's car was parked in the driveway with her cell phone in it. However, when did Jessica go to the Cooper house, and what did she do when she arrived? She did not knock on the door. She did not speak with Brad or any neighbors. She would have just driven over to the house, looked in the car, and driven off. How would these actions have assisted in locating Nancy? They did not at all. They would have been just another in a line of strange actions by Jessica surrounding Nancy disappearance.

Though it was not exactly clear whether Jessica claimed Nancy's phone was in her car or in the house, she seemed to indicate that it was in her car. As it turned out, Nancy's phone was inside the Cooper house. This was supported by Brad's statements and by Officer Daniel Hayes who was first on the scene for the Cary Police Department. Both indicated that Nancy's cell phone was in a drawer in a credenza in the foyer.cclxxxiii

If Brad did not tell her about the phone, did Jessica see Nancy on the morning of July 12, 2008, after she left for her run? Though we do not know the circumstances of this encounter, Jessica knew Nancy did not have her cell phone with her. Jessica thought the fact that Nancy did not have her phone with her would be construed as suspicious by the police. Jessica may have known that Nancy did not have her phone, but she did not know exactly where her phone was located.

It was most likely either in the house or in her car. Probably to perpetuate the strain between Brad and Nancy, Jessica felt that Nancy's phone's being in her car was more plausible. Nancy was hiding it from Brad. Jessica did not lie. She likely knew Nancy did not have her phone, but she had to guess at its location.

Jessica dropped overt hints geared toward casting suspicion on Brad. Jessica made statements such as, "…assuming her husband's telling the truth…," and "Well, this is what her husband said."[cclxxxiv] Jessica consistently conveyed to the operator information about Brad which was designed to instill doubt in the truthfulness of his statements.

During the call, Jessica relayed to the operator Brad's statements regarding Nancy's running with her friend Carey. Jessica was not aware of these plans. She also indicated that Brad's calling her was very odd. However, Brad called her to get Carey's number because he was trying to find Nancy. Why would this be odd to Jessica? The operator followed by asking if Jessica ever met Carey. In a rather unusual response, Jessica stated that she had never met Carey, but that she knew she existed. Again, Jessica was not sure if the operator believed her. Jessica tried repeatedly to establish trust throughout the call.

Jessica ended the call by telling the operator she was going to run the trails near Lochmere Drive in an attempt to find Nancy. Yet, rather than look for Nancy, Jessica drove directly over to the Cooper's house, arriving even before the police. The operator also instructed Jessica to call back in 30 to 45 minutes, but she failed to do so.

Twice during the call, Jessica utilized past tense in reference to Nancy. Jessica stated, "…contact details for her friend

Carey um that he that Nancy *had* often run with in the mornings..."cclxxxv Jessica also stated, "...I just know that she's Nancy's friend...she *used* to run with her, about a year."cclxxxvi Referring to someone who was missing in the past tense was a huge red flag. People often subconsciously utilize past tense because they know the person is already dead. *Something Brad never did.* It is unnatural for them to refer to someone in the present tense when they know the person is gone. Jessica seemed to possess information regarding Nancy's whereabouts and condition that no one else knew at the time.

Jessica could argue that she was implying that Nancy and Carey no longer ran together as of July 12, 2008. They were running partners in the past; however, this was not the case. During her court testimony, Jessica spoke of Nancy running with Carey within the last week or two of her life. Jessica expected to run with the two of them right around the time Nancy went missing.cclxxxvii Further, Carey and Nancy had plans to run the following day as well.cclxxxviii Nancy and Carey were still active running partners, a fact Jessica was well aware of. Jessica may have referred to Nancy's running in the past tense because Jessica already knew Nancy was dead.

Jessica desperately needed Nancy to be reported missing in order for the police to get involved. Since Brad was more inclined to actually look for Nancy than report her missing only hours after she had left the house, the task fell to Jessica. She was able to utilize the call as a forum to pass a tremendous amount of information into law enforcement's possession under the guise of being the *concerned friend*. Unfortunately for Jessica, many things about her call pointed toward the fact that she knew more about Nancy's disappearance than she overtly stated. Jessica did not call the police to report Nancy missing. She called the police to incriminate Brad in what she may have known was a homicide. The call was filled with inconsistencies, fabrications and signs of potential deception throughout. Jessica's use of the past tense when referring to Nancy's running presented the idea that she already knew Nancy was dead. Almost nothing Jessica said conveyed the belief she thought Nancy was alive. How was Jessica in a position to know these things?

Immediately after the call to the police, Jessica and her friend, Mary Anderson, raced over to the Cooper residence. After arriving, Jessica testified: "…And the first thing I did was look into Nancy's car, which was parked in the driveway. And I looked in the passenger side window and saw her bag and saw her cell phone sitting on the seat."[cclxxxix]

During her earlier call to the police, Jessica told the operator that Nancy's cell phone was in her car parked in the driveway. As discussed previously, there was no reasonable way for Jessica to know Nancy's phone was in her car when she made the call to the police. Either way, her first instinct was to look in Nancy's car to validate something she supposedly already knew. Nancy's phone was not in her car, which was even more perplexing. It was in a drawer in the foyer.

Officer Daniel Hayes of the Cary Police Department was the first police officer to arrive at the Cooper residence. Jessica told him that Brad may have had something to do with Nancy's disappearance.[ccxc] Brad arrived shortly thereafter with the two girls. He walked Officer Hayes around the exterior of the house and then through the interior of the house. As people began to gather around the Cooper front yard, Jessica began telling people of her belief that Brad was responsible for Nancy's disappearance. At this point, Nancy had only been missing for several hours. Her absence could have still had a logical explanation. Notwithstanding other possibilities, Jessica conveyed what should have been unsubstantiated accusations against Brad. Though many in the crowd also had similar beliefs, Jessica appeared to be the de-facto leader of the cause.

Jessica proceeded to assist the official investigation by informing the police of her theories regarding Brad. Though the culmination of her analysis consisted of, "I just knew," it did not stop her from insinuating Brad may have done something to Nancy. Most of the initial information she provided to law enforcement was geared toward incriminating Brad, not finding Nancy. As a matter of fact, Jessica did almost nothing to find Nancy.

Whether Jessica's statements altered the police's perception of Brad or merely validated their own conclusions, the police found a lot of Brad's initial behaviors to be suspicious and unusual. However, they failed to identify anyone else's behavior as suspicious. And the police failed to identify actions consistent with one believing Nancy was already dead, when she was only missing, as suspicious. Brad never conveyed such behavior, but it could be argued that Jessica Adam did. During cross-examination, an attorney asked Jessica about her activities on the afternoon of July 12:

Defense attorney: You were talking with other people about your beliefs about what might have happened to Nancy?

Jessica Adam: *Long pause*...I don't believe ever standing around just generally having conversations, as I testified, I was consumed with trying to locate Carey Clark or her phone number...[ccxci]

Jessica did not answer the question in the negative. She stated, "I don't believe," which was a weak assertion. As people often do in order to disassociate themselves from a statement, Jessica failed to use the pronoun "I" when referring to her actions and statements. Jessica also placed parameters around her answer in order to be technically correct. She was not standing around, which was likely a true statement. Jessica was frantic. Further, she stated she was not "*generally* having conversations." *Generally* means for the most part or more often than not. By utilizing *generally*, she actually stated that most of the time she was not standing around having conversations, but some of the time she was. She followed with the phrase, "as I testified," which meant she was not stating what happened on July 12, but she was referring to previous testimony, which provided her with additional wiggle room in her response.

The defense attorney continued the questioning:

Defense attorney: You don't recall making accusations about Brad having harmed Nancy?

Jessica Adam: I do not. I had made the call to the police at that point though. So that my, while at [sic] while standing there, the call had already been made. The people standing there were aware of the fact I made the call.

As opposed to Jessica's previous answer, she directly denied this assertion. Though she exhibited some signs of stress and distancing, it appeared Jessica did not use the word "harm" while talking to people outside of the Cooper house. Most likely, Jessica made numerous incriminating comments about Brad, but she did not state that she thought he had harmed Nancy.

Though most of the people gathered seemed to have beliefs similar to Jessica's, one bystander, Mike Hiller, did not. Mike approached Jessica and questioned her alleged plans to have Nancy paint earlier in the morning. He had spoken to Nancy the evening prior, and she agreed to watch the girls while he and Brad played tennis at 9:30 a.m. on Saturday morning.[ccxcii] He did not believe Nancy would have agreed to stay home and watch the girls if she had already agreed to paint at the same time. The defense attorney asked her about this discussion:

Defense attorney: You recall having a confrontation with Mike Hiller that afternoon?

Jessica Adam: I recall speaking very briefly with Mike Hiller as he rode by on his bicycle, yes.[ccxciii]

Though she acknowledged remembering the conversation, Jessica's response belittled the conversation. She stated that she spoke to him "*very* briefly" and added "as he rode by," which implied he did not stop during their conversation. It was a short conversation. Jessica described Mike as "vulgar" to further discredit him. Jessica encountered many people sympathetic to her theories, but Mike was not one of them. He threatened to undermine Jessica's assertions.

> Defense attorney: And he [Mike Hiller] discussed your painting plans that morning?

> Jessica Adam: I believe so, but I cannot attest to exactly what he and I spoke about.

Jessica remembered the conversation, though she attempted to downplay her memory by stating that she "believed so." She wanted to avoid answering questions about the conversation. She utilized the word *exactly* to make her statement factually correct. She remembered most of the conversation, but she did not remember *exactly* what was said. As the questions continued:

> Defense attorney: Do you remember making that statement [Brad did it] to other people?

> Jessica Adam: No, I do not…It really wasn't important at this point [that Hiller thought her painting plans were suspect].

Based on Jessica's direct response, she did not use the phrase "Brad did it" during the afternoon of Nancy's disappearance. Although she may have been doing everything she could to convince people Brad had done something to Nancy, she did not specifically state that *Brad did it*. This made sense because few knew what *it* referred to at this point.

As the missing person inquiry turned into a murder investigation, Jessica's role became more prominent and official. She was a great source of information for the police. Unfortunately, many of her statements ultimately misled the police. The Cary detectives' inability to know when people were being forthright versus deceptive significantly hurt them throughout the investigation. Many of Jessica's assertions could have been validated, but the police and prosecutors chose to believe her.

On cross-examination the following exchange took place:

> Defense attorney: You said you knew every time Nancy ran?

> Jessica Adam: I didn't say I knew every time she ran…She almost always included me in the weeks leading up to her death in the runs, specifically the runs with Carey Clark because she was trying to be inclusive…[ccxciv]

Jessica demonstrated signs of stress in this response. Once again, she put the information in the wrong order in her response. The phrase "in the runs" was in the wrong place in her statement. It should have been earlier in the sentence for it to make sense, as "up to her death in the runs" does not make sense. However, there was a bigger issue with Jessica's statement. It was factually incorrect. Not only had Jessica never run with Carey Clark prior to Nancy's death, she had never even met her. By moving around the parts of the statement, somehow Jessica internally justified that her statement conveyed some facet of truth. Nancy likely did almost always include Jessica in activities. Nancy liked to be inclusive of her friends. She also likely told Jessica she wanted her to run with Carey Clark. All three of these statements were likely true, but none of them indicated that Carey, Jessica, and Nancy regularly ran together prior to her death. Jessica had never run with Carey, not one time. Jessica badly wanted to provide evidence that Nancy's running on Saturday morning without telling her was incomprehensible, though nothing she said indicated this was the case.

Jessica's misleading statements continued. She also tried to implicate Brad through the laundry detergent *Tide*. In the early morning hours of July 12, Brad went to the local grocery store, Harris Teeter, on two separate occasions. During the second trip, Brad purchased *Tide* laundry detergent and juice. One component of the State's theory involved Brad's going to Harris Teeter merely to establish an alibi. In order to corroborate this theory, the police looked to invalidate the items Brad purchased as unnecessary or irrelevant to the Cooper household. One such item was the purchase of *Tide*.

Jessica Adam stepped forward to assist the investigation. Jessica told the police that the Coopers used *All* detergent exclusively. She claimed they used *All* because of allergies.[ccxcv] Even though the police and prosecution had years to verify

Jessica's claim, they failed to do so. She was subsequently asked a question during the trial, which resulted in her affirming her earlier statement regarding the Cooper's use of *All*. During cross-examination, the defense presented a copy of the Cooper's loyalty rewards statement from BJ's Wholesale Club, which clearly showed the Coopers purchased *Tide* almost exclusively.[ccxcvi] This was not a difference of opinion; Jessica was wrong. Her *memory* regarding the laundry detergent was incorrect. Though her supposed second-hand information, what Nancy told her, of the Coopers' laundry habits should have prompted the authorities to follow-up on the potential lead, it definitely should have been eliminated once the facts were gathered. The prosecutors and the judge allowed speculation on the part of a witness to be used as evidence. Essentially, rumors were allowed to flow into the courtroom before the defense team was able to set them straight. Someone within the police department and/or the district attorney's office either failed to do their homework or intentionally chose not to follow-up on this portion of their theory, as the value of the perception outweighed the factual circumstances.

Nancy's potential sexual indiscretions were quite taboo during the investigation and murder trial. Understandably, she was the victim. There was no need to speak poorly of her. However, one or more of her sexual indiscretions may have resulted in her murder. Unfortunately, they needed to be investigated and assessed. At least one of Nancy's sexual indiscretions was known to her circle of friends, including Jessica. Within Lochmere, there appeared to be countless other affairs taking place, and undoubtedly some of them included her friends and acquaintances. Many of the affairs overlapped and crossed each other. Nevertheless, during an interview with the police, Jessica Adam stated that she would, "…bet her life that Nancy never had an affair."[ccxcvii] Though Jessica may not have known about Nancy's earlier affairs, she was definitely aware of at least one inappropriate relationship.

In May of 2008, less than two months before Nancy died, Jessica attended the birthday party of Theresa O'Driscoll. During the party, Nancy showed another mutual friend, Michelle Simmons, a text she received. Nancy told her it was from "her man." When Michelle looked at the text, it was from a man named "Brett." Michelle showed the text to Jessica and asked her why her husband was texting Nancy. Jessica was hysterical. In response, Nancy told Jessica the message was from Brett Wilson, a former boyfriend from Canada, not her husband. Regardless, Jessica was very upset with Nancy.[ccxcviii]

Jessica told the police that she would bet her life that Nancy had never had an affair, but she was aware Nancy had some level of involvement with a man named "Brett" just two months earlier.[ccxcix] Jessica knew Nancy was at the very least acting inappropriately with a man other than Brad. As with many of Jessica's statements, she attempted to guide the investigation in the direction she saw fit. One area Jessica wanted the police to avoid was Nancy's sexual relationships. She may have been protecting the reputation of her dearly departed friend. She may have thought it had nothing to do with her death; therefore, she chose to protect her. However, if this were the case, then Jessica intentionally withheld information from investigators. Jessica could have also been protecting someone with whom Nancy was having an affair. Of course, this begs the question, who would Jessica want to protect?

Jessica must have known the person(s) with whom Nancy was involved would not come forward. If he came forward, it would have completely discredited her statement. She had to be assured he would not undermine her. He could not tell the police of his relationship with Nancy, even though this may require him to lie to the police. He could have deceived the police in order to prevent the information from affecting a current relationship, similar to what John Pearson did/claimed. People lie about affairs all the time. Nonetheless, it would have been a significant assumption to make if Jessica was not well acquainted with him. If the person having an affair with Nancy were involved in her death, it is unlikely he will ever willingly come forward.

Many of Nancy's friends went to great lengths to incriminate Brad and protect her reputation in death. Jessica, by far, did the most to convey the image of Brad as the perpetrator. Jessica directed the police toward Brad. It is hard to imagine how Jessica's errors, misstatements, and deceptions were not intentional. And the police went right along with Jessica's statements. They were completely duped by the Cary housewife. She helped provide the tunnel vision on Brad. In order to keep the focus solely on Brad, other avenues had to be discredited quickly. The idea of Nancy's having been promiscuous while she was married to Brad had to be eliminated. Though Jessica may have been trying to keep the focus on Brad, she may have also been protecting someone with whom Nancy likely had an affair.

Chapter 13 – Personal Knowledge

Jessica and Brett Adam married in November of 2002. At the time of Brad's murder trial, Brett worked as the chief technology officer (CTO) for the technology company rPath.[ccc] Brett has over 25 years of technology experience across many platforms and with various companies. He has co-founded four companies. Recently, Brett was the senior vice president (SVP) of strategy for CA Technologies in Framingham, Massachusetts.[ccci] Brett has extensive expertise within the computer and technology arenas.

Jessica was central to the entire investigation into Nancy's disappearance and murder. Brett's role, however, was not as apparent. Brett submitted an affidavit as part of the custody case for the Cooper children. He stated he had, "...personal knowledge regarding the circumstances surrounding Nancy Cooper and Brad Cooper's marital situation."[cccii] Notwithstanding his assertions, the only knowledge he provided through his affidavit was information Nancy or Jessica told him. He also included the statement in his affidavit, "I believe that Brad installed a VOIP phone system in his home..."[ccciii] It was not a statement of fact, but a hypothesis Brett crafted based on information shared with him. It provided no actual information. Brett was not able to provide statements of facts for which he could attest. He provided hearsay.

As a result of hearing regurgitated conversations from Jessica or comments from Nancy, Brett felt sorry for Nancy. It upset him enough that he felt he should provide any information he could, even if it was purely speculative. He seemed genuinely concerned about a woman who was a friend of his wife's.

During the 2011 murder trial, the State called Brett as a witness to help validate Jessica's assertions that Nancy was supposed to paint at their house on the morning of July 12, 2008. Though Brett attempted to convey a relaxed approach in his testimony, he exhibited signs of stress. When he was initially asked about what he did on the morning of July 12, he responded with a question.[ccciv] Answering a question with a question can often indicate stress or is utilized by the person as a delay tactic. The prosecutor asked Brett 32 questions while he was on the stand, and he responded to a question with a question three times. The first time was most likely a clarification because the question was confusing in reference to some equipment Brad gave him. The second time was in response to the question of July 12. This question was not confusing. The prosecutor directly asked Brett what he did on the morning of July 12.[cccv] This question was the primary reason Brett was asked to testify. He was there to corroborate Jessica's statements about what took place on the morning of July 12. He knew this question would be asked, and he had likely prepared an answer. Regardless, this question stressed him.

Brett responded to a question with a question for a third time when the prosecutor asked him what he noticed about his wife's demeanor on the twelfth of July.[cccvi] Jessica was quite upset during the day. She was much more excited and nervous than the situation should have warranted, and Brett likely knew it. This question also stressed Brett although the question was not confusing or even unexpected. Brett exhibited signs of stress when talking about the twelfth of July.

When Brett was asked about Nancy's coming over on the morning of July 12, he said, "I was aware she was coming to paint at some point, but I didn't realize it was quite that early."[cccvii] Later, Brett again stated that he did not realize Nancy was coming over quite so early. Brett never clarified as to when he expected Nancy, but it was not at 8:00 in the morning. Based on Jessica's testimony, she did not even get out of bed until after 8:00 a.m. on Saturday; therefore, she was likely not expecting Nancy at that time either.[cccviii]

Brett indicated that he and Jessica moved furniture in the morning in preparation for Nancy's painting. During his testimony, Brett stated that a friend of Jessica's, Kim Anderson, came over during the morning of July 12. Kim was puzzled by the furniture being in the hallway.[cccix] It was unlikely Brett fabricated Kim's comment, because someone could have easily compared his statement with Kim's. However, since the police were completely unwilling to pursue any potential lead not pointed directly at Brad, he was probably safe. Regardless, Brett's statement regarding the furniture in the hallway was most probably an accurate one.

When the prosecutor asked Brett about his activities on the afternoon of July 12, he stated, "We [he and Jessica] started talking about needing to contact others, to get the word out to try and find Nancy, literally."[cccx] At this time, the police were involved and no one had any leads on Nancy's whereabouts. Brett was taking appropriate additional steps to try and locate Nancy. Nevertheless, Brett ended his statement with a rather interesting word, "literally." The Adams planned to contact people who would *literally* try to find Nancy. This was as opposed to *figuratively* looking for Nancy. By Brett indicating that people should start *literally* searching for Nancy, he implied that he and Jessica were figuratively looking for Nancy. They were not actually searching for her. They may have been engaging in activities that could have been construed as assisting in the search for Nancy, but they were not *literally* looking for her.

During John Pearson's testimony, he stated he ran into Nancy at a Lowe's Food store near his new home. He found it odd because it was not the closest Lowe's Food to Nancy's home. Nancy indicated that she regularly shopped at this location because it was close to a friend's house that she often visited.[cccxi] Brett and Jessica lived close to the Lowe's Food location where Nancy ran into John. Were Brett and Jessica the reason Nancy was shopping at a different location? If not, who did Nancy spend so much time with that she did her grocery shopping near their home? Most likely, it was the Adams. Nancy was painting at their house and would often spend time there.

Though his knowledge was limited to what he was told, Brett stated in his custody affidavit that he had "personal knowledge" of what Nancy was going through regarding Brad. He seemed quite familiar with Nancy's situation. Though there was no evidence Brett and Nancy were anything more than friends, Nancy did tell people she was involved with a man named "Brett." Furthermore, if the possibility of Nancy and Brett being romantically involved was such a remote option, it should not have gotten such a strong reaction out of Jessica when she thought, supposedly incorrectly, that Nancy and her husband were exchanging inappropriate texts.

The last call to Nancy's cell phone prior to her disappearance was from Brett Adam's cell phone, late on the evening of July 11.[cccxii] Jessica claimed to have made the call, but there was limited information corroborating her assertion. There were many questions left unanswered regarding the nuances of the relationships between Brett and Jessica and Nancy.

Chapter 14 – No Justice for Nancy

Nancy's body was discovered next to a cul-de-sac off of Fielding Drive two days after she went missing. She was lying face down in a drainage ditch. She was presumed to have been dumped in this isolated location after she was murdered. The police never seemed to question whether or not the murder could have taken place at this location.

There was nothing in the autopsy to indicate Nancy's body was moved post-mortem. There was no mention of lividity on her posterior side. Lividity is the settling of blood within the body once the heart stops beating. Nancy's body was found face down. If Nancy's body had been moved or transported after death, the presence of lividity on the posterior or sides of her body would have been likely. The medical examiner, Dr. Butts, did not identify posterior lividity or any other indicators of post-mortem movement of the body in the autopsy report. Absent of any suggestion of post-mortem repositioning of the body, the most logical conclusion was that the body had not been moved.

A woman leaves her home to go jogging, and she is later found unclothed and murdered. The woman was likely either sexually assaulted or engaging in sexual activity when she was killed. Though it could have been concealed by the infestation, the autopsy presented no findings of sexual assault. There was nothing to indicate a brutal fight occurred. Other than the cause of death, there were no other injuries or significant bruising. Furthermore, most rapists are not murders.

Under a rape or attempted rape scenario, Nancy would have been abducted in one location in public in broad daylight, transported to another, and then killed without having fought back. Rapists who kill usually utilize one of two methods: he will either brutalize the woman prior to raping and killing her, or he will bind and gag the woman prior to raping and killing her. Nancy was not severely beaten, and there was no evidence she was bound or gagged. There was nothing from the circumstances of Nancy's death indicating she was murdered in conjunction with a stranger rape. In addition, there was no increase in the amount of reported rapes in the Cary area either prior to or after Nancy's murder. The other possibility was that Nancy was voluntarily engaging in or had recently engaged in some level of sexual activity.

The cul-de-sac off of Fielding Drive was somewhat desolate in 2008. It was wooded and located in the further reaches of a new subdivision. No development had taken place on the road where Nancy was found. However, the location was by no means separate from civilization. It was surrounded by community, and it had clearly been marked for development based on the presence of a paved road and drainage ditch. This was not a location to dump a dead body if one did not want it discovered. Whoever left Nancy's body there knew it would be found. It was just a matter of when.

Nancy's body was not hidden. There was no attempt to bury it. It was not even concealed with dirt or leaves. She was lying in the open. The drainage ditch may have been full of water when she was thrown into it, but it was a *drainage* ditch. It was not deep, and the water would eventually move out of the area. The body would be found. Further, someone was bound to walk down to the end of the cul-de-sac at some point. If not, a builder or surveyor would have discovered the body when they began construction in the area.

The person who dumped her body knew it would be discovered. He (though this pronoun is used in the general sense and not necessarily in the masculine sense) was not concerned with the body's being discovered. He was too panicked to care. This was not a premeditated crime. The cul-de-sac off the back part of Fielding Drive was not a place to dump a body; however, it would have been a perfect location for an affair.

Nancy had engaged in two affairs and other affairs were alleged. At the time of her death, Nancy likely considered herself separated from Brad. She was not technically divorced, but she was moving in that direction. Most of Nancy's statements and actions indicated that she wanted to end her marriage, but based on the circumstances, it would not happen quickly. Nancy may have already moved on at some level and pursued other relationships. Though Nancy aired dirty laundry regularly and loved to boast, she did not tell people about her sexual activities. The same cannot be said for her comments regarding Brad's affair. Nancy told anyone and everyone about Brad's infidelity, since Nancy wanted to extract maximum dollars from Brad as part of the divorce. His indiscretions could cost him, but she certainly did not want her infidelity to hurt her financially. As a result, Nancy had to keep her sexual escapades secret. Furthermore, if Nancy were having an affair with a married man or someone close to her circle of friends, she would have had even more reason to have kept it secret.

If Nancy were having an affair around the time of her death, she had to have sex somewhere. She and her partner could not have sex at Nancy's house regularly, and they could not have sex at her paramour's house if he were also married or in a relationship. They had to find another place for their liaisons. When plotting out the logistics of an affair, one would like to be hidden, but most importantly, not noticed. Ideally, the couple would travel to a remote area away from people and possible distractions. This is usually not possible because it takes too much time. Unaccounted for time is a huge problem when you are engaging in an ongoing affair. Nancy and Brad had not been intimate for years; therefore, she did not need to worry about Brad's smelling men's cologne or musk on her. However, she needed to have alibis and to be able to account for her time in order to avoid Brad's suspicions. Nancy and her paramour had to find a meeting location nearby.

Many affairs consist mainly of sex; therefore, finding a reliable location is paramount. A hotel is a possibility though it provides an audit trail, becomes costly over time, and allows for witnesses. Nancy loved to spend money, but she was financially constrained at the time. Nancy was also very well known in Cary. She would have surely been noticed frequenting a local hotel in the middle of the day. This was not a viable option for her.

Another option was to park in a remote part of a busy area, such as the outer edge of a shopping mall parking lot. A location such as this would not draw attention as long as the mall/store was open. It would be somewhat private since most people park as close to a store as they can. This was also not viable for Nancy and her paramour as Nancy was too well known around the Lochmere area. Someone could have noticed Nancy's BMW X5 parked out away from all the other cars. They had to find a different location.

The cul-de-sac at the far end of Fielding Drive was the perfect location. It was close to Nancy's house, yet out-of-the way and secluded from nosey people. Nancy was likely on Fielding Drive on the last morning of her life by choice. This was not the first or even the second time Nancy had been to this location. This was a regular rendezvous point.

Nancy left the Cooper residence around 7:00 a.m. on Saturday morning, July 12, 2008 to go jogging. Nancy likely intended to jog several miles prior to meeting her paramour at a pre-determined location. Several people saw Nancy running in Lochmere. It was possible that her paramour knew she would be jogging during the morning and tracked her down, but it was more likely they intended to meet. Nancy loved exercise, especially running. As much as she may have wanted to see her paramour, she would have also ensured she completed a run. She told Carey Clark the day prior that her legs were tired, and she chose not to run on Friday. Even if her legs were still tired, Nancy would have wanted to log a few miles on Saturday, as most long-distance runners feel they have to run regularly to in order to maintain their conditioning. This provided a perfect alibi for her. Brad would reasonably assume a two hour run based on Nancy's long runs, but with the fatigue in her legs, she planned to run significantly less. Therefore, she could run for about 30 minutes and then meet her paramour for an hour or more of alone time, thereby getting her home in time for Brad's tennis match at 9:30 a.m.

Based on the eyewitness accounts of Nancy's running path on July 12, there were a few places that would have fostered a good meeting place. One of the more likely places would have been Hemlock Plaza off of Kildaire Farms Road. It was approximately three miles from the Cooper residence. It provided a convenient place to wait for someone without drawing undo attention, as it was not an overly busy area, and it was somewhat concealed from the main road by landscaping. After Nancy and her paramour met at or near Hemlock Plaza, they could have driven to Brittabby Court via Penny Road to Holly Springs Road. The drive took less than 10 minutes.

Upon arriving, the couple ensured they were alone. After some initial conversation, the couple engaged in sexual activity. At some point, either during or after, Nancy was murdered. With whom did Nancy visit Brittabby Court? She could have been meeting John Pearson, though he seemed to have an alibi; however, the police never bothered to confirm it. She could have been meeting with some unknown person, which was certainly possible. The final possibility was that she met with "Brett," or as Nancy referred to him, "her man." Though Nancy could have been referring to Brett Wilson in Canada or another Brett, more than one of her friends thought it might be Brett Adam. With the excessively suspicious actions of Jessica Adam surrounding Nancy's disappearance and death, it was a possibility. Whoever she was meeting, Nancy had to have communicated with her paramour prior their rendezvous. She likely utilized email, Facebook, cell phone, or a face-to-face meeting. Unfortunately, the Cary Police destroyed her cell phone. The communication likely could have been established if the police thoroughly investigated more than one possibility in her murder.

There are various scenarios for what happened to Nancy. One possibility involved a confrontation. Potentially the spouse of Nancy's paramour or another paramour of Nancy's followed them to Brittabby Court. An argument erupted and ended with the person's hands wrapped around Nancy's neck, not letting go until she was dead. There are two reasons this scenario is unlikely. First, Nancy was almost completely naked when she was killed. If someone startled the couple while they were in the throes of passion, Nancy would have likely covered up or at least started to cloth herself as the argument began. Second, Nancy's paramour was present, and this scenario would imply he did little to protect or defend her. With another person present to run interference, there would have likely been more evidence of a struggle. The fight would have taken longer, and Nancy would have likely had more bruising and injuries on her body than suggested in the autopsy report.

Though it could have been another paramour, the likelihood it was the significant other of the person in the car with Nancy was very low. Women rarely strangle as a means of committing murder. Even if the woman was completely enraged, it was an unlikely scenario. In one study, out of 200 strangulation cases, only one case involved a female strangler.[cccxiii] Furthermore, if a woman strangled Nancy to death, one would expect to see significantly more defensive wounds on Nancy. She was in great shape and in the prime of her life. Nancy would have undoubtedly put up a fight. There would have been evidence of such.

Under another scenario, Nancy may have decided to end the relationship for any number of reasons. With the feeling of rejection hanging over him, her paramour became enraged, strangling Nancy to death before she was able to defend herself. He let his emotions get the best of him. Unsure of what to do, he pushed Nancy out of the car and into a drainage ditch next to the road. This scenario cannot be ruled out, but with Nancy's body found unclothed and the lack of additional injuries, it reduces the likelihood of this scenario.

In the final possible scenario, Nancy and her paramour were possibly engaging in some form of sexual asphyxiation, which is a fetishistic act that supposedly results in greater sexual arousal through partial suffocation or strangulation. Because of the circumstances and nature of the subject matter, the accuracy of the associated statistics is debatable, but many sources estimate that hundreds of deaths occur each year in the United States as a result of sexual asphyxiation. Though most of the deaths result from individuals engaging in choking activities alone, there have been cases reported of partner-assisted deaths. However, many of the deaths were ruled a homicide as opposed to accidental, as the person failed to admit to the sexual acts or left the scene upon the death of their partner.

In a panic, the sexual partner fled the scene. He was consumed with a multitude of emotions. He absorbed the shock and horror of realizing his sexual partner was dead, and the potential culpability of his actions. He was dealing with the fear of being charged with murder, coupled with the guilt of being responsible for a person's death. Further, the person was engaging in sexual behavior considered deviant by many. It is taboo. The person could face personal and professional shame and disgrace. It is a completely overwhelming situation where many people choose *flight*. He cannot bring back his loved one, and he must also cope with juggling self-preservation against his moral obligations.

We do not know who was in the car with Nancy. The person in the car was most probably having an affair with her. He likely drove a small vehicle with a distance width between the two tires of just 47 inches. Unfortunately, the Cary Police Department failed to compare the measurements against any other vehicles, other than the Coopers'. The person was possibly linked to Jessica Adam in some capacity, but with the convoluted relationships within Lochmere, it would be difficult to ascertain the exact connection.

During one of his interviews with police, John Pearson stated that he believed that Nancy went running with someone she was having an affair with. Jessica also speculated what she thought may have happened to Nancy, though her theory was merely alluded to during her initial call to the police. Jessica stated that Nancy went out for a run on her own and then something happened.[cccxiv] When Jessica was asked if Nancy was supposed to be running with someone else, she responded, "…he, this friend…" before changing the pronoun *he* to *she*, which lined up with Nancy's female friend Carey Clark.[cccxv] Off of script, Jessica thought that Nancy had gone running with someone male. During the call to the police, Jessica also indicated that she wondered aloud if an accident may have happened after Nancy's run. Both Jessica Adam and John Pearson had similar theories as to what Nancy was doing and what happened to her.

Whoever was in the vehicle with Nancy on the morning of July 12 had more than a slight interest in directing the police toward Brad. Was the person covering up a murder or an accident? Regardless of the initial act, an innocent woman lost her life, and the perpetrator's subsequent actions violated many additional laws through direct interference with a police investigation and tampering with computer evidence.

In 1996, a bomb exploded, rocking the Centennial Olympic Park in Atlanta, Georgia. It was immediately a high-profile case with international implications. The public wanted justice, and they wanted it quickly. The FBI initially interviewed a security guard by the name of Richard Jewell as a witness. Later, a former boss of Jewell's raised the possibility of Jewell as the bomber based on his track record as an over-zealous police officer.[cccxvi]

The FBI knew of other cases where fire fighters or police officers started fires or planted bombs in order to become the hero. Jewell fit the FBI's profile. He was former law enforcement and had bomb training. Through interviews with friends and co-workers, the FBI collected additional information validating their theory of Jewell as the bomber.[cccxvii] Some of his acquaintances even claimed he had a backpack similar to what was used in the Olympic bombing. The media fueled the fire by casting Jewell as the Olympic Park bomber.

The police knew the location from which the 9-1-1 call was made reporting the bomb. They also knew Jewell's location at the exact time the call was made. After extensive testing and analysis, the FBI determined that Jewell could not have made the 9-1-1 call. Jewell also passed a private polygraph test.[cccxviii] The FBI dismissed him as a suspect. It was later determined that the domestic terrorist Eric Rudolph was responsible for the bombing.

What if the FBI had ignored or rationalized the exculpatory evidence they discovered concerning Jewell? What if they still believed he committed the crime and the US Attorney's Office did not feel compelled to do its own due diligence? Since many people to this day still think Jewell may have planted the bomb at Centennial Park, regardless of the clear evidence exonerating him, he could have easily been convicted.

Unfortunately, the Cary Police Department and the Wake County prosecutors disregarded evidence contrary to their theory of how Nancy was killed and who committed the murder. They failed to properly evaluate Nancy Cooper's murder. They had one very compelling piece of evidence: a temporary Internet file on Brad's computer. However, almost none of the other evidence supported the computer evidence. The temporary Internet file meant premeditation of at least 12 hours, yet the prosecution's theory involved a rage killing. The search itself did not support any logical scenario for why Brad or anyone else would have electronically viewed the location where Nancy's body was eventually found. There were 16 witnesses who believed they saw Nancy jogging at a time after which the State's theory said she was already dead. There was a phone call from the Cooper home phone to Brad's cell after the time the State contended Nancy was dead. In addition, the autopsy indicated she died at least four to six hours after she last ate, which also went against their theory. The prosecution generated creative explanations for each piece of contrary evidence. There has been no justice for Nancy. Whoever killed Nancy is breathing a huge sigh of relief that the authorities were so easily duped.

Afterword

Bradly Cooper was convicted of murdering Nancy Cooper on May 5, 2011. Almost two years later, on April 9, 2013, his case went before the North Carolina Court of Appeals. The defense brought forward three issues to be heard by the Court of Appeals: 1) whether the trial court erred by preventing Giovanni Masucci, forensic expert for the defense, from testifying because of a discovery violation; 2) whether the trial court erred by significantly limiting the testimony of defense computer expert, Jay Ward; and 3) whether the trial court erred by preventing the defense from gaining access to law enforcement sensitive information.[cccxix]

On September 3, 2013, the North Carolina Court of Appeals ruled on Brad's case. The Court's three judges sided unanimously with the defense on all three motions and ordered a new trial.[cccxx] The Court of Appeals found that Judge Paul Gessner, who presided over the 2011 murder trial, had repeatedly abused his discretion.

In limiting Jay Ward's testimony, the Court of Appeals stated, "The probative value of the testimony excluded was not outweighed by the danger of unfair prejudice..." and it "prevented [the] defendant from presenting expert testimony, challenging arguably the strongest piece of the State's evidence... and requires a new trial, because there is a reasonable possibility that, had the error in question not been committed, a different result would have been reached..."[cccxxi]

With regard to the trial court preventing Giovanni Masucci from testifying, the Court of Appeals again ruled that Judge Gessner abused his discretion as the "…exclusion…was disproportionate to the purposes this state's discovery rules were intended to serve."[cccxxii] The defense was not trying to gain an advantage by calling Mr. Masucci to testify, as they were merely reacting out of necessity since the State had successfully limited Mr. Ward's testimony in a critical area.

Prior to and during the trial, the defense team requested the policies and procedures of the Computer Analysis Response Team (CART) within the FBI. The policies and procedures explained the manner in which law enforcement personnel extracted data that would later be presented as evidence at trial. The State successfully argued that providing the documents would compromise national security. Though that may well have been the case, Judge Gessner allowed the State to use the veil of national security as a blanket covering a wide range of data without even determining how or if it was of a national security nature. He took the State's word for it.

Though there is certainly a need for various data to be considered restricted and in some cases classified, it is a very troubling concept within a criminal trial. With regard to this trial, the defendant had no manner in which to question or impeach the process by which law enforcement arrived at its conclusion regarding the computer evidence. It was considered above reproach. It goes against the very principles of a fair trial and due process.

In a decision that may impact how local law enforcement agencies utilize federal government assistance in criminal cases, the Court of Appeals stated that a trial court, "must determine with a reasonable degree of specificity how national security or some other legitimate interest would be compromised by discovery of particular data or materials..."[cccxxiii] Judge Gessner allowed the State to hide behind the banner of national security. Without thoroughly reviewing the materials, the trial court had acted inappropriately.

On September 20, 2013, the Wake County District Attorney's Office, by way of the Attorney General's Office, petitioned the Supreme Court of North Carolina regarding the ruling by the Court of Appeals in the case against Bradley Cooper.[cccxxiv] Unfortunately, the Wake County District Attorney's Office stayed consistent with its disregard for actual evidence in their submission to the Supreme Court. They proceeded to present a volume of embarrassing attempts to convince the Court of the vast array of *evidence* they presented at trial, such compelling and direct links to the murder as Brad stating he cleaned his trunk after spilling gasoline weeks prior, although detectives did not smell the odor of gasoline. The State saw this as a clear link to Brad's guilt in Nancy's murder. The State failed to bring in experts to discuss the vaporization rates of benzene, the component of gasoline with the strongest smell. The State simply believed the detectives should have smelled gasoline, a lay opinion based on pre-conceived notions. How this type of conjecture could ever be considered evidence and placed in a legal document from the Attorney General's Office of North Carolina is unclear.

Continuing with the State's presentation of lay opinion on tangential circumstances to Nancy's murder, they submitted *evidence* to the Supreme Court that one of Nancy's friends said it was difficult to put on a sports bra. The clear inference was that Brad was unable to fully put on Nancy's sports bra after she was dead. Beyond the fact that this assertion proved nothing, their theory was clearly never tested. Did any of the prosecutors ever try to put a sports bra on a woman lying on the ground? In trials, the actual process took about 15 seconds. The tighter the bra, the longer it would take to slip a sports bra on a prone figure, but it is easily achievable. Why did Brad supposedly fail to completely dress Nancy as the prosecution's theory would imply? Apparently, utilizing their *logic*, Brad must have been unable to slip socks or running shorts onto Nancy, though the prosecution failed to illicit additional laypersons to assert such.

Three judges from the Court of Appeals reviewed the case thoroughly and came to a unanimous decision. However, the State's petition claimed that the Appeals Court failed to take into account the voluminous evidence the State presented in court and only acknowledged the evidence of a Google search of the area where Nancy's body was found. They went on to note that the defendant told police he cleaned areas of his house he did not clean and did not clean areas he claimed to have cleaned. Was the State suggesting this was the *compelling* evidence three judges overlooked? The State continued by noting that the defendant was an expert on VOIP telephone technology, which was somehow evidence he spoofed a call. This is the equivalent of providing evidence that the defendant was an expert shot with a rifle, while failing to provide any evidence the victim was actually shot with a gun.

The Wake County prosecutors did not stop after providing conjecture as evidence to the Supreme Court. They proceeded to lecture the Court of Appeals on its use of the term "direct evidence" versus "circumstantial evidence."[cccxxv] Though the Appeals Court misused the term "direct evidence" at one point in its report, it was debatable whether they were using the legal term or merely the more general, customary use of the term *direct*. Later in the document, the Appeals Court referred to the computer evidence as "directly linking," which was most likely what they intended in the first use. Regardless, the grammatical error had no bearing on their decision, but the State chose to address it as an attempt to undermine the credibility of Appeals Court's decision. The men and women tasked with prosecuting criminals and ensuring justice felt Brad received a fair trial. Regardless, the North Carolina Supreme Court declined to review the Court of Appeals' decision, which meant Brad was entitled to a second trial.[cccxxvi]

On September 22, 2014, Bradly Graham Cooper returned to court in Wake County to enter a plea. As if Brad was stuck in a terrible dream, the judge presiding over his plea hearing was Paul Gessner, the same judge who presided over Brad's 2011 trial that was overturned by the Appeals Court. The Appeals Court repeatedly chastised Judge Gessner for violating Brad Cooper's Constitutional rights and abuse of discretion, yet he was still allowed to oversee Brad's plea agreement hearing. Brad and his attorneys fought for years to overturn many of Judge Gessner's rulings; however, in the end, Brad landed right back where he was prior, sitting in front of the judge who was responsible for inflicting numerous injustices and Constitutional violations upon him.

Regardless of the clear bias of the judge, the proceeding commenced. After several rounds of questions regarding whether or not Brad understood his rights, he pled guilty to second degree murder in the death of his wife, Nancy Cooper. While under oath, Brad was then asked, "Did you kill Nancy and dump her body on Fielding Drive?" After a brief, private discussion among the attorneys and judge, Brad responded, "Yes."[cccxxvii]

Did Brad respond "yes" because of the requirements of his plea agreement, or did he just confess to killing Nancy? Brad provided no details or explanation for why he chose to plead guilty. Brad was sentenced to a minimum of 145 months and a maximum of 183 months, with credit for time served of almost six years or 71 months.[cccxxviii] Brad ultimately decided that spending an additional six to nine years in prison was more favorable than taking his chances with the judicial system. If Brad had even an ounce of faith left in the judicial system, it was completely wiped away as he saw Judge Gessner seated in the courtroom. Brad may have had made the right decision, at least regarding his future, but it significantly limits our ability to understand what happened to Nancy.

Near the end of the proceeding, Brad's attorney requested the State return Brad's laptop computer and cellular phone once the case had been closed. Though speculation varies, most likely, Brad wanted possession of the electronic devices so that he could have the items reviewed by experts for additional clues as to who may have tampered with his computer. Judge Gessner quickly denied the motion. He stated that the items were instruments of the crime for which the defendant had pled guilty.[cccxxix] This was the end of the discussion.

The investigation into Nancy's murder and subsequently, Brad's trial, was riddled with mistakes, errors in judgment and possibly willful misconduct. However, none of the authorities in this case seemed overly concerned. As Chief Bazemore of the Cary Police Department so casually put it, "Mistakes were made, but we learn from them and move[d] on."[cccxxx] During the plea agreement hearing, Howard Cummings, assistant district attorney, commended the work of the police in this case. Not only did Mr. Cummings fail to see any problems with the conduct of law enforcement during this investigation, he felt obligated to provide them accolades in open court. The conduct by many of the authorities in this case has never been addressed, even though they repeatedly disregarded procedures, professional standards, and ethics, all in the name of *justice*. Unfortunately, there has been no justice for Nancy, and there may never be.

[i] Miller, Laura, "The Duke Lacrosse Rape Scandal: The Definitive Account," www.salon.com/2014/04/06/the_duke_lacrosse_rape_scandal_the_definitive_account/, Salon.com, April 6, 2014.
[ii] Ibid.
[iii] "Duke lacrosse prosecutor disbarred," www.cnn.com/2007/LAW/06/16/duke.lacrosse/, CNN.com, June 17, 2007.
[iv] Ibid.
[v] Jessica Adam call to Cary Police Department to report Nancy Cooper missing, www.wral.com/news/local/audio/3250012/, July 12, 2008.
[vi] Lamb, Amanda, "Love Lies, A True Story of Marriage and Murder in the Suburbs," The Berkley Publishing Group, 2011.
[vii] City Data.com, www.city-data.com/city/Cary-North-Carolina.html, accessed April 2014.
[viii] WRAL, www.wral.com/news/local/asset_gallery/3709968/, Brad Cooper Deposition, October 2, 2008.
[ix] Christina Wells testimony, www.wral.com/specialreports/nancycooper/video/9481302/, April 21, 2011.
[x] John Pearson testimony, www.wral.com/specialreports/nancycooper/video/9502023/, April 26, 2011
[xi] Brad Cooper deposition, www.wral.com/news/local/asset_gallery/3709968/, October 2, 2008.
[xii] Ibid.
[xiii] Ibid.
[xiv] Lamb, Amanda, "Love Lies," The Berkley Publishing Group, 2011.
[xv] Ibid.
[xvi] Ibid.
[xvii] Brad Cooper deposition, www.wral.com/news/local/asset_gallery/3709968/, October 2, 2008.
[xviii] Ibid.
[xix] Alice Stubbs testimony, www.wral.com/specialreports/nancycooper/video/9397111/, April 6, 2011.
[xx] Ibid.
[xxi] Brad Cooper deposition, www.wral.com/news/local/asset_gallery/3709968/, October 2, 2008.
[xxii] Ibid.
[xxiii] Alice Stubbs testimony, www.wral.com/specialreports/nancycooper/video/9397111/, April 6, 2011.
[xxivxxiv] Ibid.
[xxv] Brad Cooper deposition, www.wral.com/news/local/asset_gallery/3709968/, October 2, 2008.
[xxvi] Ibid.

xxvii Lamb, Amanda, "Love Lies," The Berkley Publishing Group, 2011.
xxviii Jessica Adam testimony, www.wral.com/specialreports/nancycooper/video/9273562/, March 15, 2011.
xxix Ibid.
xxx Brad Cooper deposition, www.wral.com/news/local/asset_gallery/3709968/, October 2, 2008.
xxxi Ibid.
xxxii Gary Beard testimony, www.wral.com/specialreports/nancycooper/video/9372618/, April 1, 2011.
xxxiii Jennifer Fetterolf testimony, www.wral.com/specialreports/nancycooper/video/9367169/, April 1, 2011.
xxxiv Jessica Adam testimony, www.wral.com/specialreports/nancycooper/video/9269912/, March 14, 2011.
xxxv Lamb, Amanda, "Love Lies," The Berkley Publishing Group, 2011.
xxxvi Jennifer Fetterolf testimony, www.wral.com/specialreports/nancycooper/video/9367169/, April 1, 2011.
xxxvii Carey Clark testimony, www.wral.com/specialreports/nancycooper/video/9275339/, March 15, 2011.
xxxviii Jessica Adam testimony, www.wral.com/specialreports/nancycooper/video/9273558/, March 15, 2011.
xxxix Brad Cooper deposition, www.wral.com/news/local/asset_gallery/3709968/, October 2, 2008.
xl Testimony of various witnesses, www.wral.com/specialreports/nancycooper/asset_gallery/13488892/?s=1.
xli Brad Cooper deposition, www.wral.com/news/local/asset_gallery/3709968/, October 2, 2008.
xlii Diana Duncan testimony, www.wral.com/specialreports/nancycooper/video/9257491/, March 11, 2011.
xliii Donna Lopez testimony, www.wral.com/specialreports/nancycooper/video/9269755/, March 14, 2011.
xliv Mike Hiller testimony, www.wral.com/specialreports/nancycooper/video/9510146/, April 27, 2011.
xlv Emergency Petition For Writ Of Certiorari To Review Clearly Erroneous and Potentially Prejudicial Discovery Orders of the Superior Court, North Carolina Court of Appeals.
xlvi Brad Cooper deposition, www.wral.com/news/local/asset_gallery/3709968/, October 2, 2008.
xlvii Brad Cooper deposition, www.wral.com/news/local/asset_gallery/3709968/, October 2, 2008.
xlviii Ibid.
xlix Ibid.
l Ibid.

[li] Ibid.

[lii] Ibid.

[liii] Jessica Adam testimony, www.wral.com/specialreports/nancycooper/video/9275134/, March 15, 2011.

[liv] Defense closing arguments, www.wral.com/specialreports/nancycooper/asset_gallery/9537664/, May 3, 2011.

[lv] Craig Duncan testimony, www.wral.com/specialreports/nancycooper/video/9269751/, March 23, 2011.

[lvi] Lamb, Amanda, "Love Lies," The Berkley Publishing Group, 2011.

[lvii] Diana Duncan testimony, www.wral.com/specialreports/nancycooper/video/9258857/, March 11, 2011.

[lviii] Craig Duncan testimony, www.wral.com/specialreports/nancycooper/video/9269751/, March 23, 2011.

[lix] Jessica Adam testimony, www.wral.com/specialreports/nancycooper/video/9273562/, March 15, 2011.

[lx] News conference, www.wral.com/news/local/video/3207082/, July 14, 2008, 6:30 p.m.

[lxi] William Boyer testimony, www.wral.com/specialreports/nancycooper/video/9252586/, March 11, 2011.

[lxii] Christopher Hill, City County Bureau of Identification, testimony, www.wral.com/specialreports/nancycooper/video/9304109/, March 21, 2011.

[lxiii] Christopher Hill, City County Bureau of Identification testimony, www.wral.com/specialreports/nancycooper/video/9305510/, March 21, 2011.

[lxiv] William Boyer testimony, www.wral.com/specialreports/nancycooper/video/9252586/, March 11, 2011.

[lxv] Christopher Hill, City County Bureau of Identification testimony, www.wral.com/specialreports/nancycooper/video/9305510/, March 21, 2011.

[lxvi] WRAL News Conference, http://www.wral.com/news/local/video/3207082/, July 14, 2008.

[lxvii] Lamb, Amanda, "Love Lies," The Berkley Publishing Group, 2011.

[lxviii] Detective Jim Young, Cary PD, testimony, www.wral.com/specialreports/nancycooper/video/9343671/, March 28, 2011.

[lxix] Defense Closing Arguments, www.wral.com/specialreports/nancycooper/video/9541522/, May 3, 2011.

[lxx] Nancy Cooper Murder Trial, WRAL Tweets re: Untaped Testimony, http://frictionpowered.wordpress.com/file-cabinet/nancy-cooper-murder-trial/, accessed February – August, 2014.

[lxxi] Lamb, Amanda, "Love Lies," The Berkley Publishing Group, 2011.

[lxxii] Weather Underground, weather history for Raleigh-Durham Airport, July 12, 2008, www.wunderground.com/history/airport/KRDU/2008/7/12/DailyHistory.html?

req_city=Cary&req_state=NC&req_statename=North+Carolina, accessed June 2014.

[lxxiii] Lamb, Amanda, "Love Lies," The Berkley Publishing Group, 2011.

[lxxiv] Emergency Petition For Writ Of Certiorari To Review Clearly Erroneous and Potentially Prejudicial Discovery Orders of the Superior Court, North Carolina Court of Appeals.

[lxxv] Nancy Cooper Murder Trial, WRAL Tweets re: Untaped Testimony, http://frictionpowered.wordpress.com/file-cabinet/nancy-cooper-murder-trial/, accessed February – August, 2014.

[lxxvi] Defense closing arguments, www.wral.com/specialreports/nancycooper/asset_gallery/9537664/, May 3, 2011.

[lxxvii] Nancy Cooper Murder Trial, WRAL Tweets re: Untaped Testimony, http://frictionpowered.wordpress.com/file-cabinet/nancy-cooper-murder-trial/, accessed February – August, 2014.

[lxxviii] Detective Jim Young, Cary PD, testimony, www.wral.com/specialreports/nancycooper/video/9356923/, March 30, 2011.

[lxxix] Ibid.

[lxxx] Emergency Petition For Writ Of Certiorari To Review Clearly Erroneous and Potentially Prejudicial Discovery Orders of the Superior Court, North Carolina Court of Appeals.

[lxxxi] Detective Jim Young, Cary PD, testimony, www.wral.com/specialreports/nancycooper/video/9356923/, March 30, 2011.

[lxxxii] "The Day She Disappeared," Dateline, http://www.nbcnews.com/video/dateline/44208320#44208994, August 20, 2011.

[lxxxiii] Levitan, Ben, Telephone Expert's Report, In the Matter of State v. Bradley Cooper Case No. OCA 08-3863, January 29, 2011.

[lxxxiv] Garry D. Rentz, Donna A. Rentz, & Krista C. Lister v. Bradley Cooper, Consent Order for Permanent Child Custody, May 9, 2009.

[lxxxv] North Carolina Court of Appeals, State of North Carolina v. Bradley Graham Cooper, September 3, 2013.

[lxxxvi] Howard Kurtz interview with WRAL.com, www.wral.com/news/local/noteworthy/video/9563382/#/vid9563382, May 6, 2011.

[lxxxviii] Lawfirm.com, www.lawfirms.com/resources/criminal-defense/criminal-defense-case/discovery.htm, 2014.

[lxxxix] Ibid.

[xc] American Bar Association, Standard 3-3.11 Disclosure of Evidence by the Prosecutor, www.americanbar.org/publications/criminal_justice_section_archive/crimjust

standards_pfunc_blk.html, accessed May & June, 2014.

[xci] Emergency Petition For Writ Of Certiorari To Review Clearly Erroneous and Potentially Prejudicial Discovery Orders of the Superior Court, North Carolina Court of Appeals.

[xcii] Ibid.

[xciii] Ibid.

[xciv] Ibid.

[xcv] City-Data.com, www.city-data.com/crime/crime-Cary-North-Carolina.html, accessed July – August, 2014.

[xcvi] Taleb, Nassim, *The Black Swan: The Impact of the Highly Improbable*, April 17, 2007.

[xcvii] American Bar Association, Standard 3-3.11 Disclosure of Evidence by the Prosecutor, www.americanbar.org/publications/criminal_justice_section_archive/crimjust_standards_pfunc_blk.html, accessed May - August, 2014.

[xcviii] Ibid.

[xcix] Cornell University Law School, Legal Information Institute, http://www.law.cornell.edu/rules/fre/rule_404, accessed July-August 2014.

[c] "The Day She Disappeared," *Dateline*, http://www.nbcnews.com/video/dateline/44208320#44208994, August 20, 2011.

[ci] Justiceforbrad Blog, http://justiceforbradcooper.wordpress.com/2011/08/26/justice-for-brad-responds-to-dateline-nbc/, accessed February – September, 2014.

[cii] Gardner, Kelly, www.wral.com/specialreports/nancycooper/story/9309649/#iKqjoepGECx8z0vZ.99, WRAL.com, March 22, 2011.

[ciii] "The Day She Disappeared," *Dateline*, http://www.nbcnews.com/video/dateline/44208320#44208994, August 20, 2011.

[civ] Jenipher Free testimony, www.wral.com/specialreports/nancycooper/video/9391562/, April 5, 2011.

[cv] Diana Duncan testimony, www.wral.com/specialreports/nancycooper/video/9257491/, March 11, 2011.

[cvi] Brad Cooper deposition, www.wral.com/news/local/asset_gallery/3709968/, October 2, 2008.

[cvii] Detective Gregory Daniels, Cary PD, testimony, www.wral.com/specialreports/nancycooper/video/9443990/, April 14, 2011.

[cviii] Brad Cooper deposition, www.wral.com/news/local/asset_gallery/3709968/, October 2, 2008.

[cix] Jessica Adam testimony,

www.wral.com/specialreports/nancycooper/video/9273558/, March 15, 2011.
[cx] Jay Ward testimony,
www.wral.com/specialreports/nancycooper/video/9469090/, April 20, 2011.
[cxi] Lamb, Amanda, "Love Lies," The Berkley Publishing Group, 2011.
[cxii] Emergency Petition For Writ Of Certiorari To Review Clearly Erroneous and
Potentially Prejudicial Discovery Orders of the Superior Court, North Carolina
Court of Appeals.
[cxiii] Davis, Stacy, "Cooper jury not ready to share deliberations," WRAL.com,
www.wral.com/specialreports/nancycooper/story/9563005/#fkb9Bs8D2DG3ik
7m.99, May 6, 2011.
[cxiv] Gardner, Kelly, "Brad Cooper juror speaks out about murder trial,"
WRAL.com, www.wral.com/specialreports/nancycooper/story/9677512/, June
2, 2011.
[cxv] Dr. John Butts, Medical Examiner, testimony,
www.wral.com/news/local/video/9293074/, March 18, 2011.
[cxvi] Strack, Gail B., & Dr. George McClane, *How to Improve Your Investigation
and Prosecution of Strangulation Cases*,
www.ncdsv.org/images/strangulation_article.pdf, May 1999.
[cxvii] Pollanen, MS, & Chiasson DA, Fracture of the hyoid bone in strangulation:
comparison of fractured and unfractured hyoids from victims of strangulation,
www.ncbi.nlm.nih.gov/pubmed/8934706, Journal of Forensic Science, January,
1996.
[cxviii] Ubelaker, DH, *Hyoid Fracture and Strangulation*,
www.ncbi.nlm.nih.gov/pubmed/1402747, Journal of Forensic Science,
September, 1992.
[cxix] Strack, Gail B., & Dr. George McClane, *How to Improve Your Investigation
and Prosecution of Strangulation Cases*,
www.ncdsv.org/images/strangulation_article.pdf, May 1999.
[cxx] Ibid.
[cxxi] Ibid.
[cxxii] Gardner, Kelly, "Blood Found Beneath Nancy Cooper's Fingernails,"
WRAL.com,
www.wral.com/specialreports/nancycooper/story/9313873/#Q8w2opy2Xrpdv
Bqt.99, March 23, 2011.
[cxxiii] Report of Autopsy Examination, Office of the Chief Medical Examiner,
Chapel Hill, NC, Document B200803115, Nancy Cooper, July 15, 2008.
[cxxiv] Jessica Adam testimony,
www.wral.com/specialreports/nancycooper/video/9273558/, March 15, 2011.
[cxxv] Diana Duncan testimony,
www.wral.com/specialreports/nancycooper/video/9257491/, March 11, 2011.
[cxxvi] Dr. John Butts, Medical Examiner, testimony,
www.wral.com/news/local/video/9293074/, March 18, 2011.

cxxvii Ibid.

cxxviii Ibid.

cxxix Report of Autopsy Examination, Office of the Chief Medical Examiner, Chapel Hill, NC, Document B200803115, Nancy Cooper, July 15, 2008.

cxxx Christopher Hill, City County Bureau of Identification, testimony, www.wral.com/specialreports/nancycooper/video/9304109/, March 21, 2011.

cxxxi Ibid.

cxxxii Ibid.

cxxxiii Ibid.

cxxxiv Ibid.

cxxxv Probable Cause Affidavit, Search Warrant, 104 Wallsburg Court, Cary, NC, July 16, 2008.

cxxxvi Lamb, Amanda, WRAL.com, "Police Search Cary Woman's House, Vehicles," www.wral.com/news/local/story/3214017/, July 17, 2008.

cxxxvii Thomas Como, City County Bureau of Identification, testimony, www.wral.com/specialreports/nancycooper/video/9310586/, March, 22, 2011.

cxxxviii Ibid.

cxxxix Ibid.

cxl Jonathan Macy, NC State Bureau of Investigation, testimony, www.wral.com/specialreports/nancycooper/video/9316081/, March 23, 2011.

cxli The Other Side of Justice, The Brad Cooper Case, www.blogtalkradio.com/the-other-side-of-justice/2012/05/30/the-brad-cooper-case, accessed May – September 2014.

cxlii Greg Migulcci testimony, www.wral.com/specialreports/nancycooper/video/9404332/, April 7, 2011.

cxliii Defense Offer of Proof, Giovanni Masucci testimony, www.wral.com/specialreports/nancycooper/video/9518313/, April 28, 2011.

cxliv U.S. Department of Justice, Office of Justice Programs, "Forensic Examination of Digital Evidence: A Guide for Law Enforcement," April, 2004.

cxlv Computer Hope, Free Computer Help and Information, www.computerhope.com/jargon/h/hashing.htm, accessed June 2014, 2014.

cxlvi 365 Computer Security Training, "What is a Hash?" http://www.computer-network-security-training.com/what-is-a-hash/, accessed June 2014, July 15, 2010.

cxlvii Agent Gregory Johnson, FBI, testimony, 2011 trial, April 11 – 12, 2011.

cxlviii Ibid.

cxlix Kurtz & Blum Website, www.kurtzandblum.com/blog/cooper-case, accessed June 2014, June 12, 2012.

cl Defense Offer of Proof, Giovanni Masucci testimony, www.wral.com/specialreports/nancycooper/video/9518313/, April 28, 2011.

cli Ibid.

clii Gardner, Kelly, "Cooper defense attorney asked for mistrial," WRAL.com,

www.wral.com/specialreports/nancycooper/story/9464609/#qqMAd502rhf0yr
fP.99, April 19, 2011

[cliii] The Other Side of Justice, *The Brad Cooper Case*,
www.blogtalkradio.com/the-other-side-of-justice/2012/05/30/the-brad-cooper-case, accessed May – September 2014.

[cliv] Defense Offer of Proof, Giovanni Masucci testimony,
www.wral.com/specialreports/nancycooper/video/9518313/, April 28, 2011.

[clv] Gardner, Kelly, "Computer evidence at center of Cooper trial testimony,"
www.wral.com/specialreports/nancycooper/story/9426892/, April 12, 2011.

[clvi] Ibid.

[clvii] Ibid.

[clviii] Gardner, Kelly, "Brad Cooper defense questions Google Maps search,"
www.wral.com/specialreports/nancycooper/story/9440639/#k2EdXVj6fUovt6k
p.99, April 14, 2011.

[clix] Computer Hope, Free computer help & information website,
www.computerhope.com/jargon/t/timestam.htm, accessed June 2014, 2014.

[clx] Ibid.

[clxi] Defense Offer of Proof, Giovanni Masucci testimony,
www.wral.com/specialreports/nancycooper/video/9518313/, April 28, 2011

[clxii] Mueller, Lance, ForensicKB website, "Detecting timestamp changing
utilities," www.forensickb.com/2009/02/detecting-timestamp-changing-utlities.html, February 1, 2009.

[clxiii] Ibid.

[clxiv] Harrell, Corey, "Re-Introducing $UsnJrnl," Journey Into Incident Response
website, http://journeyintoir.blogspot.com/2013/01/re-introducing-usnjrnl.html, January 1, 2013.

[clxv] Ibid.

[clxvi] Defense Offer of Proof, Giovanni Masucci testimony,
www.wral.com/specialreports/nancycooper/video/9518313/, April 28, 2011.

[clxvii] What Are Cookies? Website, www.whatarecookies.com, 2002-2014.

[clxviii] All About Cookies website, www.allaboutcookies.org, accessed June 2014.

[clxix] Kurtz, Howard, State v. Brad Cooper, Kurtz & Blum website,
http://www.kurtzandblum.com/blog/cooper-case, June 12, 2012.

[clxx] Nancy Cooper Murder Trial, WRAL Tweets re: Untaped Testimony,
http://frictionpowered.wordpress.com/file-cabinet/nancy-cooper-murder-trial/, accessed February – August, 2014.

[clxxi] Hanna Prichard testimony,
www.wral.com/specialreports/nancycooper/video/9365285/, March 31, 2011.

[clxxii] Craig Duncan testimony,
www.wral.com/specialreports/nancycooper/video/9269751/, March 23, 2011.

[clxxiii] Well, Gary L., Elizabeth A. Olson & Steve D. Charman, "The Confidence of
Eyewitnesses in Their Identifications from Lineups," *Current Directions* in

Psychological Science,
www.psychology.iastate.edu/~glwells/Wells_articles_pdf/The_Confidence_of_Eyewitnesses.pdf, 2002.

[clxxiv] Ibid.

[clxxv] Liptak, Adam, "34 Years Later; Supreme Court Will Revisit Eyewitness IDs," *The New York Times*, www.nytimes.com/2011/08/23/us/23bar.html?_r=0, August 22, 2011.
Morgan III, Charles A., Gary Hazlett, Madelon Baranoski, et al., "Accuracy of Eyewitness Identification is significantly associated with performance on standardized test of face recognition," *International Journal of Law and Psychiatry*, 2007.

[clxxvi] Arkowitz, Hal and Scott O. Lilienfeld, "Why Science Tells Us Not to Rely on Eyewitness Accounts," *Scientific American*, www.scientificamerican.com/article.cfm?id=do-the-eyes-have-it, January 6, 2010.

[clxxvii] Ibid.

[clxxviii] Ibid.

[clxxix] Liptak, Adam, "34 Years Later; Supreme Court Will Revisit Eyewitness IDs," *The New York Times*, www.nytimes.com/2011/08/23/us/23bar.html?_r=0, August 22, 2011.
Morgan III, Charles A., Gary Hazlett, Madelon Baranoski, et al., "Accuracy of Eyewitness Identification is significantly associated with performance on standardized test of face recognition," *International Journal of Law and Psychiatry*, 2007.

[clxxx] Morgan III, Charles A., Gary Hazlett, Madelon Baranoski, et al., "Accuracy of Eyewitness Identification is significantly associated with performance on standardized test of face recognition," *International Journal of Law and Psychiatry*, 2007.

[clxxxi] Ford, Allison, "The Surprising Consequences of Sleep Deprivation," divine caroline, www.divinecaroline.com/self/surprising-consequences-sleep-deprivation, 2013.

[clxxxii] Schuster, Beth, "Police Lineups: Making Eyewitness Identification More Reliable," *NIJ Journal* No. 258, www.nij.gov/journals/258/police-lineups.html, October 2007.

[clxxxiii] Defense closing arguments, www.wral.com/specialreports/nancycooper/video/9541522/, May 3, 2011.

[clxxxiv] Rosemary Zednick testimony, www.wral.com/specialreports/nancycooper/video/9482132/, April 21, 2011.

[clxxxv] Ibid.

[clxxxvi] Detective Gregory Daniels, Cary PD, testimony, www.wral.com/specialreports/nancycooper/asset_gallery/9443453/, April 14-15, 2011.

clxxxvii Curtis Hodges testimony, www.wral.com/specialreports/nancycooper/video/9481741/, April 21, 2011.
clxxxviii Ibid.
clxxxix Ibid.
cxc Ibid.
cxci Rosemary Zednick testimony, www.wral.com/specialreports/nancycooper/video/9482132/, April 21, 2011.
cxcii Detective Gregory Daniels, Cary PD, testimony, www.wral.com/specialreports/nancycooper/video/9443990/, April 14, 2011.
cxciii Detective Gregory Daniels, Cary PD, testimony, www.wral.com/specialreports/nancycooper/video/9449741/, April 15, 2011.
cxciv Detective Gregory Daniels, Cary PD, testimony, www.wral.com/specialreports/nancycooper/video/9443990/, April 14, 2011.
cxcv Detective Jim Young, Cary PD, testimony, www.wral.com/specialreports/nancycooper/video/9324191/, March 24, 2011.
cxcvi Diana Duncan testimony, www.wral.com/specialreports/nancycooper/video/9258857/, March 11, 2011.
cxcvii Ibid.
cxcviii Damia Tabachow testimony, www.wral.com/specialreports/nancycooper/video/9269245/, March 14, 2011.
cxcix Detective Jim Young, Cary PD, testimony, www.wral.com/specialreports/nancycooper/video/9325961/, March 24, 2011.
cc Ibid.
cci Detective Jim Young, Cary PD, testimony, www.wral.com/specialreports/nancycooper/video/9325961/, March 25, 2011.
ccii Ibid.
cciii Flowers, Chad, "Blood found beneath Nancy Cooper's fingernails," www.wral.com/specialreports/nancycooper/story/9313873/#Q8w2opy2Xrpdv Bqt.99, March 23, 2011.
cciv Ibid.
ccv Detective Gregory Daniels, Cary PD, testimony, www.wral.com/specialreports/nancycooper/video/9444621/, April 14, 2011.
ccvi Tharrington Smith, Attorneys at Law Website, www.tharringtonsmith.com/page/alice-stubbs.
ccvii Brad Cooper deposition, www.wral.com/news/local/asset_gallery/3709968/, October 2, 2008.
ccviii Ibid.
ccix Ibid.
ccx Ibid.
ccxi Ibid.
ccxii Ibid.
ccxiii Ibid.

ccxiv Ibid.

ccxv Ibid.

ccxvi Ibid.

ccxvii Ibid.

ccxviii "Tampering allegations at Cooper Trial," abc7chicago.com/archive/8067814/, April 12, 2011.

ccxix Ibid.

ccxx Ibid.

ccxxi Detective Gregory Daniels, Cary PD, testimony, www.wral.com/specialreports/nancycooper/video/9449707/, April 15, 2011.

ccxxii Nancy Cooper Murder Trial, WRAL Tweets re: Untaped Testimony, http://frictionpowered.wordpress.com/file-cabinet/nancy-cooper-murder-trial/, accessed February – August, 2014.

ccxxiii Brad Cooper deposition, www.wral.com/news/local/asset_gallery/3709968/, October 2, 2008.

ccxxiv Finley IV, William Needham, "Hangin' with Mr. Cooper," http://www.itbinsider.com/?p=1212, May 6, 2011.

ccxxv John Pearson testimony, www.wral.com/specialreports/nancycooper/video/9501414/, April 26, 2011.

ccxxvi Ibid.

ccxxvii John Pearson testimony, www.wral.com/specialreports/nancycooper/video/9501414/, April 26, 2011.

ccxxviii John Pearson testimony, www.wral.com/specialreports/nancycooper/video/9502839/, April 26, 2011.

ccxxix John Pearson testimony, www.wral.com/specialreports/nancycooper/video/9501414/, April 26, 2011.

ccxxx Ibid.

ccxxxi Ibid.

ccxxxii Ibid.

ccxxxiii Ibid.

ccxxxiv Ibid.

ccxxxv John Pearson testimony, www.wral.com/specialreports/nancycooper/video/9501414/, April 26, 2011.

ccxxxvi John Pearson testimony, www.wral.com/specialreports/nancycooper/video/9502839/, April 26, 2011.

ccxxxvii Ibid.

ccxxxviii Ibid.

ccxxxix Ibid.

ccxl Ibid.

ccxli Ibid.

ccxlii Ibid.

ccxliii Ibid.

ccxliv John Pearson testimony,
www.wral.com/specialreports/nancycooper/video/9501414/, April 26, 2011.
ccxlv Ibid.
ccxlvi Finley IV, William Needham, "Hangin' with Mr. Cooper,"
http://www.itbinsider.com/?p=1212, May 6, 2011.
ccxlvii Jessica Adam testimony,
www.wral.com/specialreports/nancycooper/video/9269912/, March 14, 2011.
ccxlviii Ibid.
ccxlix Jessica Adam testimony,
www.wral.com/specialreports/nancycooper/video/9273558/, March 15, 2011.
ccl Ibid.
ccli Ibid.
cclii Ibid.
ccliii Cary Clark testimony,
www.wral.com/specialreports/nancycooper/video/9275339/, March 15, 2011.
ccliv Ibid.
cclv Ibid.
cclvi Jessica Adam testimony,
www.wral.com/specialreports/nancycooper/video/9275134/, March 15, 2011.
cclvii Ibid.
cclviii Carol Cooper testimony,
www.wral.com/specialreports/nancycooper/video/9510907/, April 27, 2011.
cclix Ibid.
cclx Ibid.
cclxi Jessica Adam testimony,
www.wral.com/specialreports/nancycooper/video/9273558/, March 15, 2011.
cclxii Ibid.
cclxiii Justiceforbrad Blog, justiceforbradcooper.wordpress.com/2014/02/10/red-
flags-surrounding-the-911-call-to-report-nancy-missing/, accessed February –
September, 2014.
cclxiv Ibid.
cclxv Brett Adam testimony,
www.wral.com/specialreports/nancycooper/video/9534185/, May 2, 2011.
cclxvi Jessica Adam testimony,
www.wral.com/specialreports/nancycooper/video/9275134/, March 15, 2011.
cclxvii Ibid.
cclxviii Jessica Adam testimony,
www.wral.com/specialreports/nancycooper/video/9275134/, March 15, 2011.
cclxix Ibid.
cclxx Diana Duncan testimony,
www.wral.com/specialreports/nancycooper/video/9258857/, March 11, 2011.
cclxxi Ibid.

cclxxii Jessica Adam call to Cary Police Department to report Nancy Cooper missing, www.wral.com/news/local/audio/3250012/, July 12, 2008.

cclxxiii Ibid.

cclxxiv Ghosh, Palash, "Like, Uh, You Know: Why Do Americans Say 'You Know' And Use Other Verb Fillers So Often?" www.ibtimes.com/uh-you-know-why-do-americans-say-you-know-use-other-verbal-fillers-so-often-1549810, International Business Times, January 29, 2014.

cclxxv Ibid.

cclxxvi Jessica Adam call to Cary Police Department to report Nancy Cooper missing, www.wral.com/news/local/audio/3250012/, July 12, 2008.

cclxxvii Supreme Court of North Carolina, State of North Carolina v Bradley Graham Cooper, Motion for Temporary Stay, September 20, 2013.

cclxxviii Ibid.

cclxxix Ibid.

cclxxx Ibid.

cclxxxi Ibid.

cclxxxii McClish, Mark, "I Know You Are Lying," The Marpa Group, Inc., 2001.

cclxxxiii Officer Daniel Hayes, Cary PD, www.wral.com/specialreports/nancycooper/video/9275340/, March 15, 2011.

cclxxxiv Jessica Adam call to Cary Police Department to report Nancy Cooper missing, www.wral.com/news/local/audio/3250012/, July 12, 2008.

cclxxxv Ibid.

cclxxxvi Ibid.

cclxxxvii Jessica Adam testimony, www.wral.com/specialreports/nancycooper/video/9273558/, March 15, 2011.

cclxxxviii Carey Clark testimony, www.wral.com/specialreports/nancycooper/video/9275339/, March 15, 2011.

cclxxxix Ibid.

ccxc Emergency petition for Writ of Certiorari & Motion for Temporary Stay, to North Carolina Court of Appeals, 08 CRS 22922.

ccxci Jessica Adam testimony, www.wral.com/specialreports/nancycooper/video/9274055/, March 15, 2011.

ccxcii Mike Hiller testimony, www.wral.com/specialreports/nancycooper/video/9510146/, April 27, 2011.

ccxciii Jessica Adam testimony, www.wral.com/specialreports/nancycooper/video/9274055/, March 15, 2011.

ccxciv Ibid.

ccxcv Ibid.

ccxcvi Ibid.

ccxcvii Ibid.

ccxcviii Emergency petition for Writ of Certiorari & Motion for Temporary Stay, to North Carolina Court of Appeals, 08 CRS 22922.

ccxcix Jessica Adam testimony, www.wral.com/specialreports/nancycooper/video/9275134/, March 15, 2011.

ccc Brett Adam testimony, www.wral.com/specialreports/nancycooper/video/9534185/, May 2, 2011.

ccci Brett Adam's Linkedin page, https://www.linkedin.com/in/badam, accessed April – July, 2014.

cccii Affidavit of Brett Adam, Wake County, North Carolina, July 22, 2008.

ccciii Ibid.

ccciv Brett Adam testimony, www.wral.com/specialreports/nancycooper/video/9534185/, May 2, 2011.

cccv Ibid.

cccvi Ibid.

cccvii Ibid.

cccviii Jessica Adam testimony, www.wral.com/specialreports/nancycooper/video/9273558/, March 15, 2014.

cccix Brett Adam testimony, www.wral.com/specialreports/nancycooper/video/9534185/, May 2, 2011.

cccx Ibid.

cccxi John Pearson testimony, www.wral.com/specialreports/nancycooper/video/9502839/, April 26, 2011.

cccxii Emergency petition for Writ of Certiorari & Motion for Temporary Stay, to North Carolina Court of Appeals, 08 CRS 22922.

cccxiii Murphy, Nancy, & Darren Dyke, *Strangulation in Domestic Violence Assaults*, presentation, http://www.ndhealth.gov/injury/Trainings/2010Conference/Strangulation_in_DV_Assaults.pdf September 2, 2010.

cccxiv Jessica Adam call to Cary Police Department to report Nancy Cooper missing, www.wral.com/news/local/audio/3250012/, July 12, 2008.

cccxv Ibid.

cccxvi Ostrow, Ronald, "Richard Jewell Case Study," www.columbia.edu/itc/journalism/j6075/edit/readings/jewell.html, June 13, 2000.

cccxvii "I am not the Olympic Park Bomber," CNN.com, www.cnn.com/US/9610/28/jewell.presser/, October 28, 1996.

cccxviii Ostrow, Ronald, "Richard Jewell Case Study," www.columbia.edu/itc/journalism/j6075/edit/readings/jewell.html, June 13, 2000.

cccxix North Carolina Court of Appeals, State of North Carolina v. Bradley Graham Cooper, September 3, 2013.

cccxx Ibid.

cccxxi Ibid.

[cccxxii] Ibid.

[cccxxiii] Ibid.

[cccxxiv] Supreme Court of North Carolina, State of North Carolina v. Bradley Graham Cooper, Petition For Writ Of Supersedeas And Application For Temporary Stay, September 20, 2013.

[cccxxv] Supreme Court of North Carolina, State of North Carolina v. Bradley Graham Cooper, Petition For Writ Of Supersedeas And Application For Temporary Stay, September 20, 2013.

[cccxxvi] "North Carolina Supreme Court Clears Way for Brad Cooper Retrial," ABC11, abc11.com/archive/9406098/, January 24, 2014.

[cccxxvii] Plea Agreement Hearing, Wake County Courthouse, personal notes taken, September 22, 2014.

[cccxxviii] Ibid.

[cccxxix] Ibid.

[cccxxx] "Did Someone Frame Brad Cooper?" Dare To Think, youcouldbewrong.wordpress.com/2013/09/06/did-someone-frame-brad-cooper/, September 6, 2013.

Made in the USA
Lexington, KY
18 January 2016